The Twilight of the Wild

For
Pat
Always keep the
Spirit of the Wild

The Twilight of the Wild

by

Rusty Johnson

Foreword by

Jim Fowler

Pyroclastic
Publishing

Pyroclastic
Publishing
New York
www.PyroclasticPublishing.com

Copyright © 2001 by Rusty Johnson

Cover photo: My feathered wildcat

Jim Fowler photo: Courtesy of Jim Fowler

Library of Congress Cataloging-in-Publication Data

Johnson, Rusty

The Twilight of the Wild /

Rusty Johnson.
First Printing, July 2002
ISBN 0-9715087-1-2

Made in the United States of America

The Twilight of the Wild
Dedicated to my
Mother and Father

You encouraged me to wander off the road of life and
create my own path. Whenever I became entangled in
the bambles of life, you freed me and pushed me to
continue on.

I love you both.

Table of Contents

Acknowledgments

First and foremost I must thank both of my parents, Wayne and MaryKay Johnson. They have given me a lifetime of support and sacrificed much more than they ever should have. My parents are the definition of "perfect" parents. They were always "there" whether in person or spirit.

I must also thank my mother for my life. When told by doctors that she would die if she became pregnant, due to a heart condition, she believed otherwise. My existence was planned up to the minute without a hitch, conceived on Labor Day 1970, born on Memorial Day 1971. I love you for your courage. Some believe that if she never developed a heart condition early in life, she would have developed one anyway from raising me.

I must thank my wonderful wife Melissa for her trust, devotion, and hard work. She has also lived through much of what you will read, occasionally unwillingly, yet she always trusted my vision no matter how unorthodox our lives became. If it were not for my wife's patience and dedication as a mother, these pages would still be a tree. You shall be the judge if both, my wife and the tree, made a worthy sacrifice. I also thank my daughter Ayla Rayne; she has played a large role in the creation of this book, far more than she will ever realize. Melissa and I consider her the "third prong" in our plug of life. She grounds us.

As for direct support in the development of *The Twilight of the Wild*, there is a long cast of characters I must thank for their efforts and support. I thank my grandfather Russell J. Maurer, one of the very few men carved from integrity, for offering support and belief in my work. Robert and Carol Dederick for dedicating tireless, and sometimes frustrating, hours helping to create my vision.

An extra special thanks goes to Jim Fowler for his guidance and input over the years. Sylvia Earle, Mary Cannis, Michael and Betsy Devlin, Gene Cetrone, James Gould, David Lamb, Dominic Forte, and Todd Levinson are a special few that have given me the tools to complete this venture.

I would also like to thank the individuals I have mentioned within this book, as well as the governments and organizations that allowed me to observe their worlds so closely, such as the Government of Montserrat, The United Nations, and The Endangered Wildlife Trust. Also I thank Richard Aspin and Montserrat's Emergency Department, along with Moose, Leroy, Jimmo, Wanker, Kaybee, Shot and Chicken, for their hospitality.

Last but not least, I must thank everyone within my world that I dislike. If it was not for them I would never realize how special my friends and loved ones are. Keep up the good work.

"In the end,
we will conserve only what we love,
we will love only what we understand,
we will understand only what we are taught."

- BABA Dioum

Foreword

by Jim Fowler

There are many reasons why certain people grow up with a tendency to want to work or associate their lives with the natural world, just as some children know that they want to be firemen, a pilot or an olympic swimmer. One's direction in life can often be guided by instinct from within, or from the effect one's environment such as the likes and dislike of the people around you, or from the examples set by your parents. Special experiences can also trigger a tendency to travel down a particular road in life.

In Rusty Johnson's case, he was probably guided by instinct. Knowing how he has always been devoted to learning about nature and its importance to his quality of life, there is no doubt that his devotion has been genetically programmed into his DNA. Rusty has been "hardwired" somewhere along the line to raise animals, enjoy the outdoors, and want to be an educator.

He may never know exactly how this happened. Did he get it from his parents, an uncle, an ancestor, or from one of his relatives generations ago? In my case, I became a professional trainer of "birds of prey" long before I realized that my name "Fowler" actually comes from the Anglo Saxon name that means someone who trains falcons, eagles and other birds of prey. I wrote a paper on the subject when I was in fourth grade, never knowing that I would eventually be invited by Marlin Perkins, to appear on the pilot film of *Mutual of Omaha's Wild Kingdom*, with my harpy eagle over twenty years later. I to had a compulsion to work with animals.

At a time when our world is becoming more and more disconnected from the natural world, it is critical to our future that we learn how to enable people, the voters, to care about the existence of wildlife, wilderness and open space. Not to imply that the incredible ability that we have to pursue knowledge, create unimagined technology, create comfort for ourselves and unravel the mysteries of the universe aren't miraculous and beneficial, but if we fail to learn and respect the secrets of nature that affect and control our lives, we are not as intelligent a species as we think we are.

Paul McCready, a scientist who dares to comment on the bigger picture of life and the directions in which we are going, after engineering the first human powered flying machine and solving many environmental problems through his extraordinary inventiveness, ranks "working with nature" in his book, as the number one challenge of this century. He points out that only two hundred years ago, a flick of an eyelash in geological time, nature was in control of this planet. Now, we humans are in control of nature, which is an awesome responsibility whether we understand it or want it or not. Clearly, staying connected with the world of nature today is more important than any other human endeavor, once you understand the possible consequences of our ignorance or lack of interest in the subject.

This places education and personal experiences at the "head of the class" for those people who have a desire to educate with the help of "animal ambassadors for the natural world," as Rusty Johnson does. In his book, *The Twilight of the Wild*, it is obvious that he became dedicated to sharing his love and knowledge of wildlife and the outdoors as a result of having a personal experience with animals. That is all it took for him to embark on his life's work; becoming a "spokesperson for the natural world." By doing so, he is helping thousands of people of all ages to stay connected with the importance of nature in spite of the overabundance of shopping malls, golf courses, sporting activities and other places to "hang out"; all formidable competitors for our increasingly limited leisure time. Although other people may have tried to place limitations on what Rusty could do, he never told himself what he couldn't do. There is nothing as important as first-hand experience, once you find a worthwhile path to be on. After growing up where there were a few forests and fields, he traveled to Africa as soon as he could and organized most of the trip himself - a dream come true for a naturalist. I suppose that once you have become wise in the ways of the jungle of New York City and its environs, you are more apt to be able to adapt and survive elsewhere. Africa opened his eyes even further to the meaning of nature and natural things big and small. He also, along the way, writes about the people he met from different cultures with different customs, some of whom did not think very highly of American tourists.

Rusty writes well from his viewpoint and experience, which is refreshing. Many writers believe that they must always reflect the ideas of others in order to be successful, but it is also important to combine academic knowledge with one's own personal experience in order to gain perspective to one's beliefs. Daring to draw conclusions from that which you have personally seen or heard by using your own mind, is even more important than using someone elses. As does a good sponge, Rusty soaks up information. Then, he builds upon it and delivers something of value to his audiences as does every effective writer. This is combined with a mission and messages of the future, not the past. He is a powerful spokeperson that can effect the attitudes of the public in a positive way. I hope that I have had something to do with Rusty's awareness of these messages of the future, or else I am not an effective spokesperson. I have enlisted him and the help of his animals in my lectures many times. Oddly enough, the message of the futute, in my opinion, is to not just talk about animals and how amazing they are, but to use the inherent interest in live animals to hold the attention of the audience long enough to talk about why open space, wildlife and wilderness are important to us. To put it mildly, we humans are oriented very strongly to judge the value of things within the framework of our own self interest, and if we do not explain "what's in it for us?" we may not learn to make the saving of the natural world a priority in our lives.

Adventure is another way to gain people's attention. Audiences, whether at a lecture or while reading a book, enjoy being led down an adventurous path. In fact, unpredictability in storytelling is an ancient art. Long before radio and television, it was the way information was handed down, often around a campfire. So, if you are already strongly connected to the natural world or your busy life does not allow time away from the one we have created, attend one of Rusty's lectures. Otherwise, read this book and see what it is like to embark on a road that compliments your genetic programming and benefits society as well, preferably while sitting around a campfire.

Hopefully, Rusty's book *The Twilight of the Wild*, will not be judged as just another pessimistic view of the future, but will help bring a new day and new light to all life on earth, including our own.

Jim Fowler

The Twilight of the Wild

My Apologia

"Oh no!" my mother said, while standing on our front porch, "Muffin must have killed it." As I walked out of the house to see what she was talking about, my mother pointed to a dead rabbit on the front steps, most likely killed by our pet cat. "Let me get a plastic bag to put the rabbit in, then we will bury it," my mother said as she walked into the house. At the time I was only five years old and this was my first experience with death.

As my mother searched the house for a bag, I carefully approached the dead rabbit and sat next to it. I began to pet its warm body and was amazed at the softness of its fur, even softer than any of my stuffed animals. With no visible wounds on the rabbit, it appeared to only be sleeping. It was so perfect. I had to have it.

By the time my mother returned with a plastic bag, I had already buckled our cat's rhinestone collar around the dead rabbit's neck and was dragging it around the yard by a leash. I had a pet.

"Rusty! What in God's name are you doing?" my mother yelled as she walked out of the front door. I pleaded, "Can I keep it?" My baffled mother responded, "Rusty, the rabbit is dead; you can not keep it." I then defensively replied, "It won't eat much and I will take it for a drag everyday."

Obviously, I did not grasp the concept of decomposition at that time. I could not understand why such a beautiful animal would not stay as beautiful after it had died. As you read on, you will discover I have since learned my lesson about decomposition.

After my mother convinced me that we must give the rabbit a proper burial, it was ceremoniously placed to rest in peace next to a willow tree in our back yard. Soon after the funeral I had to be enlightened on the requirements for burial, when my mother caught me burying everything I could find, whether it was dead or alive. That rabbit was my first recollection of loving "life." From then on I have been enamored with the wild creatures that share the planet and hold a curious fascination in observing how we humans co-exist with them.

During the third grade, another life altering situation occurred. While enjoying outdoor recess one spring afternoon, I was searching the school property for snakes. My grammar school sat at the base of a small mountain called Snake Hill. Every springtime, the stream that meandered between Snake Hill and my school, teemed with frogs. The immense frog population made it a prime feeding ground for snakes.

That particular afternoon it was unseasonably chilly and I did not find any snakes. But in a marshy outcrop from the stream, I found a beautiful leopard frog. As I approached the frog I noticed it was in the process of laying eggs. As she floated within a submerged tree branch she laid over 5,000 tiny black eggs which loosely attached to the twigs of the submerged branch.

As the frog continued to lays eggs, two of my classmates approached from behind and asked, "What are you looking at?"

"A leopard frog laying eggs." I responded.

"Where?"

"There", I said while pointing her out as she floated just below the surface of the water.

"Catch her." one classmate said.

While still watching the frog I replied. "It is not a good idea to pick up frogs if it is not necessary. Handling them removes a coating of slime on their skin that helps protect against virus and disease. When released back into the wild after being handled, this disturbed barrier is 'disarmed' and they can easily get sick and die."

"Well can the slime protect them from this?" one classmate yells. I turned my head toward them, confused by what he said, and saw them both hurling softball-sized rocks at the frog. Before I could respond both rocks splashed into the water, one of them on top of the frog.

Shocked by what had just happened, I quickly jumped

into the water and removed the rock off of the frog. She was dead; her flattened body floating with her string of eggs still attached to her. As the two classmates were uncontrollably laughing, I yelled, "You killed her, you stupid %@$$@%@s." Then I picked up one of the rocks and prepared to throw it at them. One classmate thought I was bluffing until I hit him in the chest with the rock. As he fell down with the wind knocked out of him, his buddy made a run for it but I was able to "peg" him in the back with the same rock. Suddenly, several teachers grabbed me as if they were the Secret Service and I had just assaulted the President of the United States.

The principal threatened me with suspension and promised to inform my mother of the violent outburst (With the zero-tolerance in schools today, I probably would have been charged with attempted murder). Although I had never been suspended in the past, I hated school and entertained the possibility of not being able to attend class with joy. Telling my mother was not much of a threat either; I felt my mother would understand my actions once she was told why I did it.

I was not suspended for my rock throwing. But the Principal did call my home, and informed my mother about her son's behavior. That evening my mother talked to me and I gave her my side of the story. She responded by saying, "I understand why you became so upset with your classmates, but I do not agree with your actions."

"Well, what was I supposed to do, they killed her!" I

sternly replied.

"Why do you love animals?" she asked while she started to prepare dinner.

"I don't know, I just do."

"How do you know you love animals?" she added.

I quickly responded, "Because the more I learn about them, the more I like being around them...And the more I am around them, the more I want to learn about them."

Then my mother said, "Some people have never learned about animals, and because they do not know anything about them, they do not care about them. Perhaps, instead of throwing rocks at the children, you could have shown them how great frogs are, and they would understand them."

With that advice I returned to school the following day armed with a field guide and not a rock. By the time recess came, I had most of the class prepared for their first wildlife expedition. That day my classmates and I spotted more than three different species of frog and counted over thirty frogs within a half-hour. Two weeks later, I amazed both of the "reformed frog squashers" when I brought them back to the scene of the crime and showed them the dead frog's eggs as they began to hatch.

I have not kept in touch with those two classmates but I am sure they remained "reformed frogs squashers." When I thought about it later, I realized it was not only them killing the frog that bothered me, it was the fact that the children who did it were both normal everyday kids with great acceptance among their peers. One would expect such actions from the "troubled classmates" but from normal everyday children? Unfortunately, ignorance has no prejudice, and will afflict anyone who allows it to exist within them.

Throughout my school years I not only tried to learn all I could about the natural world, but I felt great accomplishment when I transferred the wonders of nature to people not yet connected to it. This passion developed throughout my school years and became a vital support when school became difficult.

As I previously mentioned, I hated school. This strong negative emotion towards standard academia was well earned; I have Dyslexia and Aphasia. Both of these "disabilities" affect one's ability to read and remember information. I was not diagnosed until my last years of high school. Before then, teachers were generally unaware of learning disabilities, so I was more generically labeled as "lazy, not applying myself, and not trying hard enough." While in grammar school, my parents noticed I was having learning problems, but when they approached my teachers about it many stated, "Oh Mr. and Mrs. Johnson, don't worry about Rusty, he is a good kid." And my parents replied over and over again, "Yes, we know he is a good kid, but he can't read, write, or spell."

Because I never lit fires on school property or flushed M-80's down their toilets, I was pushed through barely passing by the skin of my teeth. I received little extra help or support from my school system, with the exception of several very caring and dedicated teachers with whom I have remained friends to this day. I will admit I sometimes was my own worst enemy. I did not want to admit I had a "problem" and would rather not hand in an assignment at all if I knew all the answers were wrong.

It was my mother who tirelessly worked with me to help me get through school. Sometimes, with me wearing headphones to block out any "distractions", we would read through my homework assignments by taking turns one sentence at time so I would not become too tired and frustrated. She brought me books on any subject I even showed a remote interest in and tried to get me to read, read, read. In time, read I did if it was about nature. When I would get frustrated with myself, she would tell me, "You are not stupid, you just have to find another way to learn."

Then on June 25, 1989, after countless opinions, tutors and meetings with teachers, student counselors, doctors, allergists, and optometrists my parents consulted with, a miracle happened; I graduated high school. I was so tired from celebrating my accomplishment the night before, I ended up on the front page of our city newspaper, in my cap and gown with my chin on my fist; sleeping. The caption below the photo read, *Graduate Rusty Johnson in his thinking pose.* I can just imagine what some of my teachers were thinking too! Graduating was a high point of my life after 12 years of "confinement" I was now free. I do not think it was a high point for the school system. They did not know I graduated with a second grade reading level and I was not about to tell them. Looking back, maybe they did know.

It was through these difficult times I would find myself spending more time around animals and the outdoors. Even while attending classes, I was always known to have a snake nearby or a ferret sleeping in my book bag. It was a comfortable outlet and confidence builder, something I knew well.

During my last year of high school, I met a naturalist who lectured with his animals at schools. While working with him I became licensed in falconry (training hawks, falcons and eagles). While practicing falconry, I gradually obtained a number of wild animals and began giving lectures at schools, museums and universities.

Through the years my lecture series snowballed into a full-time business, with me conducting as many as 250 lectures per year. It became the perfect occupation. I spend every day surrounded by wild animals, while opening the eyes of thousands of people to creatures many would never otherwise see. I am my own boss, doing what I love, and I get paid for it!

As for my "job title" I consider myself more of a conservationist than an environmentalist. Much of the environmentalist movement revolves around the notion that humans are a "blight" on the earth, where the conservationist movement believes man can co-exist with nature.

Although I do agree with the former on many points, I must side with the latter. But foremost, exceeding any "job title," I am a humanitarian struggling to preserve mankind's quality of life.

This lifestyle also has provided many exciting opportunities. I have had the pleasure of appearing with my animals on the *Today Show, Late Night with David Letterman, Live with Regis and Kathy Lee,* and *Late Nite with Conan O'Brien.* I have trained a falcon for magician David Copperfield and on numerous occasions I have had the honor of working alongside Jim Fowler of *Mutual of Omaha Wild Kingdom.* He is a man who has personally enlightened my view of the natural world as well as entertained my entire family for generations via television every Sunday evening. Of course I will never forget Johnny Carson's perfect impression of Jim's "boss" Marlin Perkins. "While Jim wrestles the two-horned rhino in heat, I will make martinis for the tribe's women."

Through the years I have lived with a number of animals, hawks, eagles, owls, falcons, condors, vultures, snakes (some weighing over 200 lbs), and alligators, to name a few. I have also had the opportunity to interact on a one on one basis with other animals including elephants, tigers, lions, bears, and chimpanzees. But none of the wild animals I have ever possessed or worked with, was ever considered a "pet." They are ambassadors for their wild cousins. They are the "voice" of their species and form a connection between their kind and society.

This connection can only be achieved by a human seeing an animal in the flesh and looking into each other's eyes. That animal becomes real; its individual personality shows through and captures the observer's soul. A photograph or documentary can not achieve this.

While conducting over 2,500 lectures over the past 13 years, hundreds of audience members have asked, "Why don't you write a book?" Never wanting to respond with the truth, "I am lucky if I can read, much less write." I would simply reply, "In due time."

When I felt I was ready to write a book I began the writing process. While developing my limited writing skills, I would begin writing a book then throw it out, not because of the "technical difficulties" in writing, but because the books simply were not original. They were nothing different than what overwhelms any bookstore shelf. I did not want to write a book for the sake of writing a book.

The idea that created *The Twilight of the Wild* came to me several years ago while I was sitting on a cliff watching a crow feed her young. The crow landed on her stick nest which held her three chicks. In her mouth was an unidentifiable piece of meat which the chicks aggressively wrestled for until it was devoured. Then the mother crow flew back into the forest.

Twenty minutes later she returned to the nest with a dead snake swinging from her beak. As she landed on the nest, all three of her chicks pinched their beaks around the snake and began to brawl over it. The smallest of the three chicks was pushed aside while the two larger siblings each swallowed an end of the dead snake. After a violent tug of war, the dead snake snapped in half and they both swallowed their ends.

By the time the snake was ingested, their mother had already left to search for more food. Several minutes had passed when I saw the mother crow returning to the nest with something large in her beak. The unrecognizable prey seemed to violently flutter in the crow's mouth, yet the crow seemed to have no difficulty flying with it. When she landed on the nest I was able to see what the prey was; it was a Burger King bag.

The three baby crows squawked for food while their mother stuck her head into the bag, pulled out an empty hamburger wrapper and threw it off the side of the nest. She then would repeatedly stick her head back into the Burger King bag, grab a beak full of french fries and feed her chicks one by one. When the fries were finished, the mother crow pushed the bag off the edge of the nest. As the paper bag lightly fell between the branches below, the mother crow flew back into the green forest.

This mother crow was either heavily connected in the food industry or she discovered the Burger King bag on the side of the road, thrown out by a passing motorist. Crows in general, are extremely intelligent and opportunistic feeders, taking advantage of almost any possible food source. Yet, the thought of a crow associating a paper Burger King bag as a possible source of food, made me realize that we are living in *The Twilight of the Wild.*

As we begin the 21st century, we enter a time where the modern world is expanding at its greatest rate ever. As our human demands expand, so do our "habitat" demands. Consequently, we are losing our wild lands day after day, as well as our precious wildlife. For the past 200 million years, the average rate of extinction was roughly 90 species per century. Currently we meet that number every two weeks.

We must ask ourselves, what kind of life do we want for our children and grandchildren? Quality or quantity...a garden or a junkyard.

Do we want to create a world full of concrete and steel, people crammed next to one another, noise deafening our living space while polluted air continuously attacks our lungs with every breath and our polluted waters poison our children? Or, with consideration and effort, would you rather create a world where nature and man coexist in a symbiotic relationship, a balance benefiting both, resulting in the best of both worlds. If the world were footwear, would you prefer to walk on Birkenstock sandals or flip-flops?

If this trend continues, as it appears it will, it means that today is the best it is ever going to be. My daughter's generation will have a poorer quality of life than my wife and I have had and our future grandchildren's quality of life will be even poorer.

In addition, as third-world cultures and governments

strive to get their piece of the action, the flames of conflict are fueled. Like over crowded animals, we battle for ownership, territory, and resources. Because human behavior is so similar to "animal" behavior and plays such an overwhelming role in our quality of life, I include the human animal in this book many times over. Because of my fascination with this reality, I decided to study and experience *The Twilight of the Wild* for myself and pass the adventure on to others. That is what this book is about. This is not a scientific evaluation of our future nor a manifesto of an impending doom. Above all, this books aims to entertain, and if it opens minds or encourages people to appreciate life, all the better. And in response to all those who inquired, "Why don't you write a book?" The time is due...

Welcome to *The Twilight of the Wild.*

The Twilight of the Wild

Chapter I

Trespassing

It was early in the morning and a thick film of dew coated the overgrown grass. My socks became drenched with water as the sun began steaming the night's moisture off the ground.

My German shepherd, Raven, sat anxiously beside my truck as I walked into the hay field with my peregrine falcon perched on my fist. The falcon's name is Frightful, after the falcon in the book *My Side of the Mountain*, by Gene George Craighead.

Frightful is an experienced flyer as well as a proficient hunter. His claim to fame is flying directly into a flock of starlings and coming out the other side with a bird in each foot.

Like a boxer warming up for a title fight, Frightful began to beat his wings faster and faster as I walked him into the field. I gently raised my fist to the sky and he took to the air. While flying wide circles around me, he rose higher and higher until he gained over 500 feet in altitude, or "pitch," which is the falconry term.

The field had a slight incline to it and at the top of the hill was a small pond which flocks of ducks frequent. Also known as the Duck Hawk peregrine falcons are exclusively adapted for hunting other birds.

My plan was to have Frightful at a high pitch, then signal him to fly over the pond. While at the same time, Raven would run up over the hill and jump into the pond.

When Frightful reached about 700 feet he began to "wait-on" which is the term for hovering overhead in a single place, like a Harrier jet. This let me know that he was ready to go. As I walked up the incline, I signaled Frightful to follow. Raven was whining with anticipation while he awaited his command. "Come!" I yelled, and Raven bolted across the field towards the pond. German shepherds are not your typical bird dog, nor did I train him to be one. He just loves to swim and all I need him to do is to startle the ducks into flying. A one hundred-pound German shepherd belly flopping into their pond always seemed to do the trick.

Frightful was in perfect position when Raven leaped over the bank and into the water. After hearing a large splash, a small flock of mallards launched towards the sky. All six of them bolted over the field in a tight flock. I looked at Frightful and he had already locked-in on the flock and began to "stoop." A stoop is when the falcon turns upside down, folds it wings back against its sides and dives headfirst towards its prey. This position allows the falcon to mimic the form of the most aerodynamic shape in nature, a raindrop.

Amazingly, seconds before a stoop, peregrines must precisely gauge and predict where the location of impact will be. Otherwise they will have to break out of their stoop in order to steer and drastically lose their speed.

The peregrine falcon is the king of speed. Considered the fastest animal on earth, a team of German scientists has clocked a peregrine falcon diving at an astonishing 217 miles per hour.

As Frightful was stooping, the mallards quickly noticed him and dropped their altitude, barely skimming over the grass. Instinctively knowing that falcons prefer to hunt in wide open space, ducks will try to escape by taking cover or flying close to the ground to discourage the deadly dive. If the same ducks were pursued by a raptor that was better suited to hunt in the deep woods, such as a goshawk, the ducks would respond by trying to make a break for the open air and field.

During the chase, all that could be heard was the frantic flapping of the ducks wings along with the faint whistle of Frightful's bells cutting through the air. When diving at such high speeds, the small bells on Frightful's legs used to keep track of him, no longer ring. The intense downward fall causes the metal bead within the bells to lay pinned against a single side and the bell becomes more of a whistle.

As Frightful gained on the flock, the ducks tried to muster all the speed they could. Suddenly, the flock broke apart. Four flew straight into the forest for cover while the other two pulled upwards and tried to drag race the falcon over the trees.

Frightful singled out one of the two mallards by slightly shifting his wings. Then, like an anti-aircraft missile, Frightful collided with the duck raking both of his feet across its back. After the point of impact, Frightful streaked past him like a fighter jet to bank a turn and finish the job. While the duck spun out of control they both disappeared out of sight.

If he killed the duck, it is common for a larger wild hawk to show up and try to kill the peregrine while stealing the duck. So as Raven continued to swim, I quickly jogged over to the edge of the field where I saw the falcon and the duck collide.

There was no sign of either of them. Except for a few small duck feathers softly rolling over the grass as the wind blew them, it appeared as though the whole situation never took place. The lucky duck must have escaped. This was not a surprise; catching prey is not an easy task for any animal, especially for a creature on the top of the food chain such as a falcon. Roughly, eight out of every ten falcons in the wild die before they are one year old, mostly due to starvation. It keeps their population in balance, much as falcons aid in controlling the populations of other birds such as ducks.

I was slightly concerned that Frightful was missing. Several years prior, he chased a flock of birds and became lost. Three days later a Game Warden found him and tracked Frightful's leg-band number back to me. When I received the phone call telling me that he had found my falcon, I responded, "Thank you for finding him, I will cruise over and pick him up. Where are you located?"

"Baltimore, Maryland", he responded.

"What!"

It was a seven-hour drive to pick him up and he had flown the three hundred and fifty miles in only three days. That is three days of flying during daylight hours only; falcons are as blind as humans at night.

With no sign of either of them, I returned back to the middle of the field and began to swing my lure. A lure is a ball of leather that is tied to the end of a six-foot cord. I trained Frightful to chase it by tying pieces of meat to it.

With no response from the swinging lure, I quickly spun it six or seven times and threw the entire lure into the air. Then over the horizon, a tiny spec began to rapidly enlarge. I picked up the lure and continued to spin it from its cord. Frightful approached 500-feet overhead, "waited-on," then dove straight down at me while rapidly giving a single corkscrew twist to move his feet into attack position. He streaked past me like a bullet and tried to snatch the lure from the air, barely missing it. He then quickly banked a tight turn and attacked the lure again. This time, after making contact with it, he fluttered down to the ground and began to eat the meat. I sat on the ground next to Frightful as he devoured his food. Raven returned from the pond, shook the water out of his fur, and lay down next to us.

There are references to Caesar using falcons to destroy pigeons carrying messages and falconry was reputedly the favorite sport of almost every king of England. During the Middle Ages falconry was taken very seriously. There evolved a social custom in falconry by which birds of prey were allocated to a rank. A man could not own a bird which was a higher rank than himself. For example, only an emperor was allowed by law to have an eagle. If a lower class of individual was guilty of possessing an eagle, the punishment could be as severe as getting a hand cut off. If one was charged with shooting a bird of prey, they may have been subjected to getting their eyes poked out. But before falconry was considered a luxury art form, it was simply a way for one to put food on the table before gun-powder was invented.

Although falconry is taken less seriously in today's

world, a falconer's role and responsibility towards his or her bird has always remained as involved and intense.

"I think I would like to take up falconry as a hobby", many have people said to me. I responded to them all with the same remark, "Don't". If one thinks falconry is simply a hobby, they have a lot more learning to do. Falconry is not a hobby nor is it a sport. Hobbies and sports can be concluded and pushed aside until the next time one has the desire to play again. Falconry is a preoccupation, a full-time responsibility. A King's Chief Falconer could never have more than two alcoholic drinks during dinner in fear he would become drunk and neglect to properly care for his birds. .

As Frightful was finishing his food, a huge red-tailed hawk swooped down barely over our heads. I slid my body closer to Frightful to convince the red-tail not to dive down and try to kill him. A red-tailed hawk would not think twice about diving down and killing a much smaller "intruding" peregrine.

This was her territory and as far as she was concerned we were intruding. She was an adult female red-tailed hawk. This was evident because she had a brick red tail and chocolate brown eyes. Juvenile red-tails have brown tail feathers and yellowish eyes. Also, when she buzzed over us she belted out a raspy adult scream like a steam whistle,

Keeeeeeeerrrrrrr.

She was obviously a female because she was so large. With most birds of prey, the female is larger than the male. The size difference between sexes provides a broader range of possible prey species for a pair of hawks rearing young.

The smaller male can dispatch smaller more agile prey which would be too fast for the larger female. The female can prey upon more larger robust animals that would prove too large and powerful for the male to catch. Also, if there is a shortage in prey of one size or another, the dimorphism (size difference) between the pair gives them alternative food options.

While Frightful was finishing up his meal, the red-tail continued to pass overhead screaming in protest. Frightful became uneasy about the lingering hawk and dragged the lure beneath my bent knees as I sat on the ground. Under the cover of my legs, he continued to feed while occasionally peeking his head up between my knees to make sure the red-tail was not too close.

With every flyby, the red-tail got closer and her screams more intense. I understood why she worked so aggressively to defend her territory; it is prime real estate. Red-tailed hawks control a territory of about 2-3 square miles. Their habitat is commonly an open field with bordering forests, but they can also be found perched in the tree lines along large roads and highways. Red-tailed hawks are easily spotted by their signature whitish chest and spotted brown bellyband.

The red-tailed hawk is one of the most common North

American hawks. I have seen them flying over the lonely plains of Montana's Big Sky country as well as preening their feathers while perched on a lamp post along New York City's Bronx River Parkway.

Red-tails have such a successful population, that they are now at a "saturation point" in some areas. This means that every possible territory that could be suitable for a red-tail, in now occupied by one. From an ecological perspective the "saturation" of red-tailed hawks is marvelous and promising for the future of their species. But for the individual red-tailed newcomers born every spring, it is an overwhelming obstacle to face.

From the very moment a red-tail hawk emerges from its shell, it is in a race with time. Its body must grow to full size, its feathers must completely develop, and it must begin to fly and hunt, all within a matter of 15-20 weeks. If the parents fail to provide a sufficient food supply, the young chick may kill its own brother or sister to survive. If all these physical needs are not completely met, the hawk will die within the first few months of its life. But leaving the nest is only the first step in the life long marathon of survival.

After a red-tail leaves or "fledges" its nest, the search for a territory begins. This is especially difficult for the "saturated" red-tail. The "rookie" juveniles are violently forced out of every prime habitat already claimed by the more experienced adult. They are then forced to occupy nothing but second-rate territories harboring a poor food supply. These territories are proven second rate because there is not a red-tail already there prepared to protect it. As these young birds resort to occupying less suitable territories, their worries are not over. They are inexperienced hunters with unconditioned muscles and limited flying skills. These realities are the nails that seal the coffins of over 80% of the red-tailed hawks born every year.

Whenever a red-tail comes into a human's view, it should be appreciated and revered. The brilliant brick hue of adult tail feathers hang as a badge of honor: they are survivors, the elite within their species.

After Frightful gorged himself full of food, he hopped up on my fist and wiped his beak clean on my glove as we walked back to the truck. Raven ran ahead of us to declare his "shotgun" seat, while the red-tail continued her aggressive campaign against us.

By the time the three of us were settled in the truck, the red-tail flew high up onto the tip of a tall evergreen. Like a motionless royal guard, she silently stared at our truck as it slowly rolled down the dirt road, never unlocking her piercing stare until we were deep within the forest and out of sight.

Chapter II

El Spirit que limpia la tierra
(The Spirit that Cleanses the Earth)

"Excuse me sir, my condor is on your roof." These words sounded crazy coming from his 18-year old neighbor. But he was wondering what was stomping around on the top of his house.

My neighbor followed me outside to see Elwood, my condor, perched on top of his chimney. With feathers measuring longer than a human arm, he held out his 10-foot wingspan resembling an ancient idol. For hundreds of years many native cultures revered the Condor as having supernatural powers. Many thought the Condor was a flying spirit that cleansed the earth of impurities.

Elwood flew up on my neighbor's roof after a long afternoon of leaf-diving. Every year as I rake the yard's fallen leaves, he jumps from my front porch, roof, or a tree, directly into the pile of leaves. He then proceeds to jump up and down while flapping his wings, which re-disperses the leaves throughout the yard giving the appearance that it had never been raked. But for an animal that has the ability to fly at an altitude of over 16,000 feet, I was thankful he was just wandering on the neighbor's roof.

I walked into my neighbor's backyard, whistled to attract Elwood's attention, then I threw his "green bowl" high in the air.

Elwood's green bowl is very special to him. It is nothing more than an old chewed up Tupperware salad bowl, but since he was a young chick, I have always fed him from the same bowl. Whenever he flies out of sight, a single throw of the green bowl from the roof of my house brings him back home.

When I threw the bowl, Elwood jumped off the chimney after it. With four powerful flaps of his enormous wings he aimed his course, then glided towards me. His wings casted a giant shadow over the lawn like a B-1 bomber, and with the grace of a hang glider, he touched down to earth with his wings stretched out, then awkwardly ran to a stop. He laid on his belly with his wings flapping by his sides, and with a series of friendly grunts and hisses, he solicited for food as if he were still a young chick. I filled his bowl with four pounds of chicken gizzards, which he promptly devoured within fifteen seconds.

I thanked my neighbor as he curiously observed from a distance, then I walked back toward my yard. Elwood followed closely running with his wings spread out to his sides like a child pretending to fly.

He then quickly hopped up on the porch and perched on the railing to preen his feathers while I attempted to finish raking the yard.

Elwood is an Andean condor, one of only two species of condor in the world, the other being the California condor. The Andean condor is larger than the California condor, which makes it the largest bird of prey in the world, and the second largest flying bird in the world. The largest flying bird is the wandering albatross. This huge gull-like bird only beats out the condor in wingspan by three inches on each wing.

Andean condors are found mainly in Venezuela, Colombia, Chile and Argentina. They soar on the trade winds scavenging for food such as beached whales along the South Pacific coast as well as patrolling for the deceased along the Andes mountain range.

Elwood was hatched by the United States Fish and Wildlife Service. Born at the Patuxent Research Center in Maryland, he took part in the early stages of the California condor recovery program. Andean condors were used in a pilot program to learn condor breeding and hatching techniques.

The two species of condor are so similar, that Andean condors were released in potential California condor release sites. In case there were any unforeseen "mishaps" in the early stages of the project, the limited California condor population would thus not be wasted. The Andean condor is also endangered, but they were not nearly as rare as their Californian cousins were at the time.

Ten thousand years ago, the California condor roamed as far east as New York. But during the European migration towards the American west, the condor's habitat and food supply was destroyed. The large herds of grazing animals, such as the bison were wiped out, shot simply for their tongues and hide. The very lead bullets that killed them, poisoned the scavenging condors.

By 1980, only thirty California condors lived in the wild. Seven years later on April 19th, the last free-flying representative of its species was captured. Adult condor #9, or AC-9 as it was called, was destined for Los.Angeles Zoo, making the California condor's captive population twenty-seven, and its wild population zero.

Plans were not made to utilize Elwood after the hatching experiment was concluded. So I then received him as a gracious gift from a former colleague. Several weeks old at the time and no larger than a softball, he resembled a space alien. The dark wrinkled skin of his bald head loosely hung behind his oversized beak, contrasting his orange mouth that he would gape open whenever wanting to be fed.

Condors stick their heads inside dead animals to feed, so their heads are bald. If they had feathers on their head, it would become a disgusting mess. Also, the ultraviolet rays from the sun beat down on the bald head killing any germs or bacteria that might collect there. The fleshy inside of an Andean condor's mouth is orange. Most birds that have an orange mouth also have a liver deficiency, yet it is the common color for a healthy condor.

Even at such a young age he seemed to inhale food by the pound. If in the wild, his natural mother would first cut his food into little pieces by eating it. Then she would "throw it up" as she fed the chick, not something I was willing to do, especially since he likes to eat dead rats.

We compromised. My mother's blender quickly became off-limits so I was forced to do it by hand with a good pair of scissors.

Few know the disciplined art of cutting dead rats into little pieces. If not done properly, one will be there all day and end up with only a ruined pair of scissors and a dead rat that looks like it was run over by a truck.

At first I did feel quite cruel whenever preparing Elwood's meals. But since it was the closest way to duplicate what Elwood's mother would do for him in the wild, I quickly got over it.

Condors take about six-months to fledge, and within that time period, Elwood slowly began to take shape. His dark fluffy downy feathers were gradually being replaced with stiff gray feathers that held tight against his body streamlining him for flight.

Elwood has accompanied me on over two thousand lectures, enlightening the minds of over 500,000 audience members, many of whom would never have the chance to see such an animal, much less in such an intimate setting. I believe each one of those people reserved a corner of their mind to preserve his image knowing one day they may say to their grand-children, "I actually saw one of those...but they don't exist anymore".

I have been approached by people that have met Elwood during a lecture over ten years prior and they still remember him as if it were yesterday. Yet, they do not remember what they had for lunch that day.

Sometimes meeting Elwood can prove too intense for an audience member. He has caused people to uncontrollably wet their pants on several occasions. It became such a common occurrence, I now forewarn audience members of the fact and recommend they "contain" themselves.

The overwhelming reactions people have towards Elwood proves the importance in protecting something so wonderful. Of course, telling people we should save wildlife is nothing new; that has been the agenda of many people for the past 100 years. I have seen aisles of books in bookstores that repeat the same message like a motivational audio tape.

For the past 200 million years, the average rate of extinction was roughly 90 species per century. Now we meet that number every two weeks. In the United States since 1973, there has been over 1,000 species listed as endangered. Only about 20 of those species have been officially improved. That may be 20 species that might not exist today if not for human intervention. However, if a professional baseball player had that average, he would be flipping burgers for a living.

Hundreds of governments and private organizations are dedicated to the preservation of every species imaginable. Then why do we have such a poor track record?

Because too many times, the success of an endangered animal is measured by the population of that species. That is the first battle, but only a small part of the overall war. These populations are also subject to natural disasters such as hurricanes, disease, and other unforseen catastrophes.

Creating and saving its proper habitat is equally important. What is the sense of saving an animal that has no place to live once it is saved? This was a concern for some very passionate people when AC-9, the last California condor in the wild was captured. Destined for Los Angeles Zoo, it had to be re-routed to the San Diego Wild Animal Park because protestors had chained themselves to the Los Angeles Zoo's front gate.

Many people feel that the California condor should die with dignity. They believe the condor is a dinosaur of the past, and would have disappeared by now from natural extinction if we did not "play god and meddle".

Unfortunately, due to the California condors ability to

fly hundreds of miles in a single day, they have been known to occasionally leave the protected habitat and cause trouble. One complaint was of several young condors raiding a McDonald's dumpster.

Also, local, state, and federal governments must communicate with each other. Yes, I said government and communicate in the same sentence. It is possible, and it is vital. If one hand does not know what the other is doing, all the effort invested will be wasted.

I have seen the waste in New York State. Millions of dollars and thousands of man-hours were invested to release peregrine falcons within New York City. It was hoped that they would thrive in the city by feeding on pigeons and nesting on the buildings and bridges. It was a wonderful success. But for several years I have witnessed government work crews painting the city bridges during the falcon's peak nesting time. I have watched adult falcons standing on top of the bridges screaming in protest as the workers stare and point at them. I have been told that the peregrines have abandoned these important nest sites on several occasions. When these nest sites become abandoned, our efforts to save them are wasted.

But most important of all is public compassion. You can spend your entire life living in the forest researching what species of tree branch a monkey uses to scratch its back, but that will never save them. What is the value of one's discoveries, if there is nobody at home who cares?

This was evident during the "war" over the spotted owl.

First of all, there was never a war. In order to have a war, both sides must have some slim chance of winning. In no way will an owl be victorious over thousands of lost jobs. Unfortunately, economics makes the world go round. People must be convinced that a thriving forest is worth more than if it were destroyed. Until then it will remain a losing battle. Today, a wildlife preservationist must be a salesperson and public relations representative, more so than a scientist or researcher.

The only way any animal or other natural resource can be successfully protected is by exposing it to the general public, but not solely by technologically created media such as books, television, and the internet. The information and experiences within those media is tailored and pre-packaged, ready for immediate consumption. They are certainly priceless forms of reinforcement and "mental maintenance," making us aware of our world within the comfort of familiar surroundings. But it should never become the substitute for the true experience. There must be a more magnificent personal experience in order to spark the passion that will keep the flame of concern glowing.

Humans are a visual species. Dramatic experiences are most remembered and associated with what one sees. Hearing and smell are also great reminders and enhance the memory but sight still plays the major role within the brains memory. How much evidence can be clearly explained to a person? If not seen with our own eyes, doubt can always be created; we witnessed this during the O.J.

Simpson trial.

With all the current controversy involving the damaged ozone layer, I would venture to say people would be more concerned if the ozone's hole could be seen as a dark blackspot ominously hanging over all of our heads.

Along with my other "ambassadors," Elwood continues to be an ambassador for his wild cousins, completing a connection from which most people believe they are far removed. The truth is, none of us are.

Now twelve years old, Elwood weighs almost 25 lbs, stands four feet tall, and has a wingspan of ten feet. His overwhelming size intimidated NBC's *Today Show* Bryant Gumble into refusing to be in the same studio with him, while a brave Katie Couric conducted the interview. He has graced the stage of the Waldorf Astoria's Ballroom, and while appearing on the *Dick Cavett Show*, Mr. Cavet commented, "It is as if I am standing in the presence of a mythical god".

As the degradation of our planet coincides with the slipping condor populations, perhaps they are "El Spirit que limpia la tierra", the spirit that cleanses the earth.

Chapter III

My Feathered Wildcat

I entered the flight chamber and approached my male owl as he stood on his favorite perch. I offered him a dead rat for breakfast and he reached out with his beak pulling it from my hand. Like a parrot, he grabbed the dead rat with his right foot and held it in front of him as if holding an ice cream cone. Then after a moment of studying the rat like a fine diamond, he bit into it and swallowed it whole.

I attempted to feed the female owl, but I could not find her. Concerned that she was sick or dead, I nervously searched for her. She was nowhere to be found. I then placed a small ladder up against their nest box to see if she was in it.

Owls do not have the instinct to build a nest; in the wild, owls generally steal nests from other birds or make use of a hollow tree.

A year prior, I built them a nest box but they never used it, and sometimes seemed to avoid it. When I climbed to the top of the stepladder and peered into the hole, there she was crouched in the corner. Startled by my sudden appearance, she flinched and then hissed at me. Occasionally referred to as "feathered wildcats," owls hiss like a mad feline when they are startled or defending themselves.

She was a European eagleowl, one of the world's largest species of owl. Her six-foot wingspan fanned out to her sides made her appear even larger as her snapping beak echoed like firecrackers inside the box. Posing in a defensive posture, she stared at me with her human-sized pumpkin orange eyes and followed my every move.

I reached out to feel her "keel". The keel, also known as the breastbone, holds most of a bird's fat reserves. This is the first place I look when checking the health of any bird. If the breastbone feels sharp and I am able grab it between my index finger and thumb, the bird is too skinny, and perhaps sick. If it is difficult or impossible to grab the keel, the animal is nice and fat. This does not always mean it is healthy, but is a good indicator if it is not.

As my hand slowly reached towards her, she reared

backwards and spread her head feathers out like a cobra's cape. Then after wailing a high pitched screech protesting my intentions, she bit me on the wrist.

With a beak powerful enough to snap the neck of a woodchuck, she latched on and held tight. I sat frozen for a moment hoping she would let go, but she would not.

My only hope was to try and pry her beak off my wrist. But when I reached my free hand out, she shot her right leg out from under herself like a spear and dug all four of her inch and a half long talons into my fingers. Her rear talon stabbed me between my pinky and ring finger, clear through and out the opposite side of my hand.

As if wearing a medieval torturer's handcuffs, both of my hands began to throb and bleed. Like all raptors, an owl's foot is designed like a ratchet that can lock tight like a vice grip whenever needed. It is their instinct to squeeze harder if the prey or threat squirms and fights. Unable to move, I was forced to grin and bear it.

Surprised at her aggression I softly said, "It's okay girl, I just wanted to see if you are feeling well." She angrily twittered and squeaked while continuing to hold on with all of her strength.

Knowing I had a better chance in freeing my hand from her mouth rather than her foot, I slowly began to twist my wrist out from her beak. The more I twisted the harder she bit. Like playing tug-of-war with a fishhook, we struggled back and forth until my skin gave way with a blunt snapping sound. Satisfied that she had taught me a lesson, she immediately released my other hand.

As she settled back into her squatting position I noticed the reason for her defensiveness; she was sitting on an egg. Immediately I jumped off the ladder so as not to disturb her any longer.

I was ecstatic that they had bred, not only for the sake of possibly hatching a baby owl, but it also proved that the owls were perfectly comfortable with their living conditions. If they had any form of stress or uncertainty about their surroundings, they would have never attempted to reproduce.

I watched the owls from a comfortable distance for about ten days, only approaching to give them food and water. By the tenth night, the female seemed to spend most of her time outside the nest box. Nervous she might have been neglecting her motherly duties, I decided to intervene.

Early the next morning I looked into the chamber to see the female perched in the high corner. With her back to me, I climbed up to the back of the nestbox and opened a small door which I had built for this very purpose. As I slowly opened the door, I shown a small flashlight into the nest and saw five eggs. They lay in a tight bunch and were cold to the touch.

My initial thought was to exchange the eggs for golf balls, assuming she would soon discard them when they did not hatch. But instead I decided to put a chicken egg in the nest. I then carefully carried the owl eggs to the house and put them in a warm incubator.

After two days of incubation I "candled" the eggs. Holding an egg up to an intense beam of light makes it possible to see the shadow of the chick inside. Originally candles were the light source, hence the name "candling." Today there are machines specifically made for candling eggs; but I have never used them; holding the egg up against the lens of a slide projector does just as well.

Unfortunately the first four eggs were infertile. But as I lifted the fifth egg to the light I saw a baby owl the size of a dime, a web of blood vessels glowed around it as it fed life to the developing embryo. I placed the fertile egg back into the incubator, then tossed the four empty eggs into the woods to treat the local raccoons.

About two weeks had passed after placing the chicken egg in the nest when I saw something that almost knocked me off the ladder. Standing beneath the owl stood a proud baby rooster. She had incubated it enough to hatch it out and as of that moment seemed pretty content in caring for the hatchling. I tossed a few handfuls of chicken feed on the bottom of the nest box, and the rooster wandered about scratching and pecking the floor while "mom" stood guard.

The following morning, I returned to feed the rooster and thought tragedy had struck. The rooster was slumped over in the corner of the nest, covered head to toe in blood.

Did they finally realize it was a chicken and had killed it? Neither owl was in the nest box at the time so I reached in and removed the rooster.

As I grabbed the chick it began to squirm and kick until it slipped out of my hands and dashed across my backyard like a roadrunner. "Well, I guess you're not dead, little man." I laughed. He burned rubber across my driveway, then tucked beneath a bush.

I reached beneath the bush and pulled him out. After carrying him over to an outside hose, I rinsed him off and searched for an injury. He did not have a scratch on him. I looked at his face and noticed he had a mouthful of white hairs. While pulling them out I realize what had happened to him. The owls tried to feed him a rat. Not knowing how to react to getting pieces of rat shoved down his throat, the poor chick became exhausted and became covered in rat blood during the process.

Remarkably, the owls truly thought that no matter how ugly this "owl" was, they would still take care of it. Owls will never think twice about eating a baby rooster, yet they will gently care for that same animal if convinced it is theirs. Needless to say, I had a rooster that could have used years of serious therapy.

As the owl chick continued to develop within the egg, I candled it everyday to observe its growth. I also began to cup the egg between my hands and hoot to it. An owl's senses mature and brighten much like a light bulb on a dimmer switch and soon the owl would begin to hear my hoots through the egg's shell.

After the twenty-ninth day of incubation, when I cupped the owl egg in my hands and hooted to it, the chick hooted back! The sound was more like a kitten meowing rather than an actual hoot, but it was a definite response. The chick had now developed enough to begin leaving the egg. I carefully returned the egg to the incubator and kept a close watch on it. By evening the owl began to "pip," which is when they poke the first hole in the egg with their beak. Early the next morning the owl hatched from his egg as I held him in the palm of my hand.

Like an alien emerging from its spaceship after landing on a new planet, the owl chick kicked the last piece of shell from its wet feeble body. Totally helpless and shaking he looked like two wet cotton balls glued together. The larger of the two on top representing his gigantic head, which uncontrollably wobbled on a thin pencil neck.

Over the years I have had several eagleowls, as well as many different species of owl. One pair of owls no larger than a can of soda lived free in my bedroom for years. But, this particular owl is very special because it is totally "imprinted" to me, which means that according to him, I am his mother and I am also an owl. He feels perfectly comfortable around me just as a house cat would be to its caretaker.

This has given me the rare opportunity to learn first hand much about the hidden world of owls. Even to this day he teaches me more than I could ever learn from a textbook. He grew up in a hand-made nest situated beside my bed, and by jumping on my back as I slept, he would playfully tug on my ears with his beak to wake me for his night feedings.

Throughout his first weeks he had a voracious appetite and grew like a weed. He ate twice as much as his parents did when he was only the size of a softball. Within eight weeks, he grew from two inches tall to twenty inches tall, and by then was as big as his father but still looked like a fuzzy Muppet character.

As he continued to grow, he began exercising his wings and gained coordination. No bird "learns" how to fly - it is instinctive. But they have to learn how to maneuver and land. So his first attempts at flying looked somewhat silly. He was clumsy, and awkwardly flung his body from branch to branch. But with a couple weeks of practice he gained perfect control of his body and began to answer his primal urge to hunt.

On one particular night, I walked into the woods with the owl on my fist. It was late winter and the full moon reflected off of the snow, illuminating the entire forest with a warm glow.

As I cast the owl off of my fist, he flew up into a giant oak tree. Perching on a thick branch that reached thirty or forty feet into the forest, he stretched out both of his wings, then settled them in close to his sides. I never actively push him to hunt; I would much rather quietly stand by and see how he naturally acts. This usually means watching him sit like a statue most of the time, then occasionally hop to another branch for a better view of the forest. He did just that for about an hour when I noticed he heard something behind him. He spun his head 180 degrees and bobbed it up and down to locate the sound's direction. Then, in a single motion, he turned himself completely around and swooped off the perch towards the forest floor.

When I caught up to him he was on the ground with his feet deep into the snow. As I knelt next to him, he revealed a six-inch long spotted salamander in his foot. I offered him a piece of steak which he promptly traded for the salamander.

Unbelievably, the salamander lived through the ordeal without a scratch. The owl's feet were so big that his talons completely wrapped around the salamander instead of killing it.

How he captured that tiny amphibian is a real miracle. Yellow-spotted salamanders hibernate beneath the snow in the winter. Alcohol and proteins in the blood keeps them from freezing. Spring was near, and the salamander began to lethargically move beneath the snow as the temperature warmed. This was enough movement for the owl to locate the salamander's exact position and capture it. Not by sight, but by sound. The owl never even saw the salamander until after he captured it.

Three-dimensional hearing is what makes owls achieve the seemingly supernatural ability. Their radar-like hearing can detect sounds ten times fainter than the human ear can detect.

Several unique adaptations make three-dimensional

hearing possible. The most noticeable adaptation is the owl's face. Unusually wide and round, these facial disks are adapted to funnel sound waves much like a satellite dish.

One ear opening is higher than the other, plus one ear is a round hole while the other is a slit. This adaptation aids in pinpointing the direction of its prey. Owls also have a moveable flap of skin controlled by muscles around the ear opening. This flap protects the ear and concentrates sound waves coming from behind.

Soft modified feathers called auriculars surround their ears. Auriculars lack "barbules" allowing a clear path for sound waves. Barbules are the parts of the feather which zip together to make it wind resistant.

To provide the perfect listening environment, an owl's wing feathers have a soft covering of fuzz over them that muffles any flapping sounds during flight. This fuzz gives the owl the ability to fly silently like a moth. Not only does this allow the owl to track the hidden movements of its prey, but also gives it the ability to sneak up on its prey.

Owls can also see ten times more detail than a human during the day and equally as well at night. Their eyes are adapted to detect extremely low levels of light. Even the darkest nights holds some level of light, sometimes undetectable to us but not to owls.

They detect this faint light because of an overwhelming thickness of receptors within the eye called rods. Rods are light detectors; humans have them but not nearly as many, which is why we are blind in the dark. But unlike owls, we have additional receptors called cones, that detect color. Owls are color blind; which is a common trait among nocturnal hunters.

Also, the behavior of their pupils aids in their night vision. In the dark their pupils expand, just as ours do to allow more light in. But an owl's pupils expand the entire diameter of the eye to let as much light in as possible. So an owls eyes are completely black at night. They essentially become two wide open "black holes," drawing in as much light as possible.

It is a myth that owls never blink. As a matter of fact, they blink more proficiently than humans. Owls have three eyelids, one eyelid blinks down, much like a human eyelid, another lid blinks from the bottom up and a third eyelid, called a nictitating membrane, blinks sideways much like a windshield wiper. The extra eyelids give the much needed protection to their sensitive eyes. When owls attack prey, their eyelids shut a split second before impact in order to protect the eyes. They also use their lids to protect their eyes while feeding their young. Despite an owl's acute eyesight, they have trouble focusing on things extremely close to them. So the blurred vision of a baby owl may cause it to mistakenly peck the parent's eyes while being fed.

I have never seen an owl sleep. Any owl I have seen that looked asleep was dead. During the day, owls hide and try to be concealed, but they are always fully aware of what goes on around them. I have lived with owls for over twelve years: never once have I seen one sleep.

The saying "the wise old owl"- don't believe it. Owls are not very intelligent. People have assumed they were smart because their eyes face the front of their head resembling a human. It was commonly thought that "anything that looks human must be smart." I am sure anyone reading these pages can think of several "humans" that might disprove that belief.

But do not be tricked into thinking owls are stupid. Quite the contrary, owls are so superbly adapted for survival that so called "intelligence" is of no use to them.

Owls dominate the night. Like ghosts they silently weave their way in and out of the forests giving only the slightest glimpse to few humans. Ounce for ounce, one of the most powerful animals on earth, they are perfectly adapted for a life cloaked in darkness. Yet even these finely tuned predators struggle day to day for survival, and only the best succeed. It is not easy to catch food with your feet. Like most birds of prey, eight out of every ten owls in the wild usually die before they are one year old. Most die at the cold and bony hands of life's supreme predator, starvation. Starvation preys upon raptors just as ferociously as raptors prey upon their own quarry. It is just one spoke in the wheel that keeps the cycle of life rolling.

As I let the owl finish its steak, I placed the salmander back beneath the snow to live out the remainder of his lucky night. Then the owl jumped onto my glove and preened his feathers back into place.

Fortunately, by having a "safety net," my eagleowl is separated from the harsh realities of nature. He flies free and hunts at will, but whenever he fails to catch food, he does not perch closer to death, he lands upon my gloved fist for a guaranteed feast.

This luxury has made him somewhat lazy. Thankfully he can not read since he is sitting next to me as I write this, but it is the truth. Many animals, including humans, have a tendency to not try as hard when things are handed to them. But within every great hunter, lies an even greater opportunist.

The Twilight of the Wild

Chapter IV

The Wanderer

The earth is overwhelmingly resilient, yet it needs to remain finely tuned and balanced. Much like an arrow nicking a branch, that slight disturbance in direction will increase in severity as the arrow flies on. Just as the smallest change in our earth's balance sets off a chain reaction far greater than we can ever expect.

When Swiss chemist Paul Hermann Müller received the 1948 Nobel Prize in physiology/medicine for his development of DDT as an insecticide, no one realized DDT was a "branch". It was not until the publication of Rachel Carson's *Silent Spring* in 1962 that suspicion grew about DDT killing more creatures than the bugs it was intended to kill.

Dichlorodiphenyltrichloroethane, as it is scientifically

referred to, rapidly contaminated the wildlife as small predators fed upon the poisoned insects, then fell prey themselves to the larger predators, causing DDT to scale the food chain until the top predators accumulated the highest concentrations of the poison. Most animals did not show any visible effects from DDT, but one creature could not be overlooked: the peregrine falcon. It is the classic case demonstrating the ill effects of human disturbance on the ecosystem

By the early 1950's the peregrine falcon became extinct east of the Mississippi River and 85% of its western population vanished. Research indicated that the widespread use of DDT was the culprit. The peregrines suffered from the poison in several ways; in some cases it directly killed them, while other falcons developed warped minds losing all ability to care for their young. But the most detrimental effect was the poison's attack on the bird's calcium production. The DDT thinned their eggshells so much that when the mother would incubate the eggs, they would crack. Tragically, the very action that had brought life to every peregrine was now sending them on a crash course towards extinction.

When scientists and falconers discovered this, they began to implement captive breeding programs. Falcons retrieved from cliff sides in western Canada where DDT had not left a scar were placed in breeding chambers. Successfully reproducing after several years, the falcon chicks were hand fed by a puppet that resembled the mother in order to keep their instinctive fear of humans which is vital to any animal being released into the wild. The project's main goal was to "hack" out the young chicks in hopes of re-establishing a wild population.

"Hacking" is an ancient falconry method allowing the falcon to learn to hunt on its own. The falcon is placed on a protected platform high on a pole or building called the hack site. Several times a day food is passed up to the platform in a fashion that gives the falcon no idea that a human is feeding it. As the bird develops, it hops around the platform flapping its wings to build its strength. Eventually the falcon will jump off the platform and take to the sky. As time passes, the falcon gets better at flying and gradually learns to hunt on its own. On the days of unsuccessful hunts, the falcon can count on returning to the hack site for a free meal. Soon the falcon will become more proficient at hunting and visit the hack site less and less. At this moment, a falconer would capture the bird and train it for falconry. But in this case, the falcons were fed until they became self-sufficient and stopped returning to the hack site.

One very vital question had to be answered. Where should they place the hack sites? When releasing any animal into the wild, there must be proper habitat with an abundant food supply. Of all the areas in which falcons would thrive, scientists decided to release them in New York City.

To most people this sounded like an outrageous idea.

Why would one ever release wild animals into one of the busiest cities in the world? But, it was a brilliant decision. It filled both criteria for release: prime habitat, since peregrines nest on cliffs and they consider the skyscrapers and bridges as perfect cliffs; and the food supply could not have been better because a peregrine's favorite food is pigeons. The city became a very successful hunting ground, more so than a country field. The buildings provide perfect cover when the falcons fly down the street pursuing prey. If they miss, the buildings hide the bird's presence from potential prey on the neighboring blocks. The falcon then can fly over to the next street and try again. In a large open field where wild peregrines naturally hunt, the prey has a chance to see the falcon coming from far away and will hide until the coast is clear.

The project was such a success that New York City now holds one of the highest concentrations of peregrines in the country. Year after year, the young radiate outward searching for new territories in Connecticut, New Jersey, and up-state New York, occupying old peregrine nest sites that have been abandoned for almost 50 years. Also, the bridges spanning the Hudson River from New York City to Albany now have peregrines nesting on them every spring.

In 1972 the United States banned the use of DDT, as did many other countries. Unfortunately, many Third World countries did not, and peregrines continue to hold the risk of ingesting poisons as they migrate outside of

U.S. territories. The word peregrine means "the wanderer" and they have been known to fly thousands of miles during migration entering lands where there are no laws against DDT.

Nevertheless, after the peregrine project was implemented many large cities throughout North America followed suit. And after being the first animal ever placed on the United States Endangered Species List in 1973, the peregrine falcon was removed from it on August 25, 1999.

This recovery has become one of man's greatest success stories about a creature that we have pushed to the brink of extinction. Realizing our faults, we have triumphed in recovering the population. This does not give us the right to rest on our laurels and believe it will always be this easy. In the case of the peregrine falcon, there was an element of dumb luck. What are the chances of ever aiding another endangered species that will thrive in a city? I doubt I will ever see cheetahs running throughout Johannesburg, South Africa.

But DDT not only affected the peregrine falcon. Another catastrophe took place on the island of Borneo in the 1960's. In an attempt to exterminate malaria, the World Health Organization embarked on a major campaign to rid the tropics of mosquitoes carrying the disease. Borneo was the target and the spraying of DDT began throughout its worst effected areas. Initially, the program seemed highly successful and the population of mosquitoes dropped dramatically. Again, the mosquito was not DDT's only prey.

A minute wasp was eradicated by the spraying; this wasp preyed upon caterpillars that lived in the thatched roofs of the local houses. With the wasp gone, the caterpillar's population exploded to plague proportions and they began devouring all the roofs causing them to cave in.

While the spraying campaign continued, a second chain of events took place. The poisoned mosquitoes were eaten by gecko lizards, which quickly became sick and fell easy prey to the local cats. As a result, the cats accumulated large concentrated amounts of the poison and began to die by the thousands, which made the rat population explode in numbers. The large masses of rats devoured local crops and then brought the island something of far greater danger than malaria, the bubonic plague. In sheer despair, the Borneo government called for cats to be parachuted into the affected regions.

As of today, malaria has returned to the island along with mosquitoes that have developed a resistance to many of the pesticides. Just as in the case of the peregrine, we got more than we bargained for. Proving that massive spraying is never a suitable answer, and other options must be explored.

Chapter V

With only his Bells

I shifted into four-wheel drive and stomped on the gas. With all four of the tires scratching for traction, the truck swung back and forth pushing its way up the steep hill.

It was at the end of a winter and I was on a road that has never been plowed called Poppletown Road. Poppletown Road is a rather famous road in my hometown. For decades the lake at the top of the road played host to many midnight high school keg parties. It is so far out of the way that police would never patrol the area. I must admit, some nights I found myself up there for one reason or another, but on this day I was taking Stoli out for his daily outing.

Stoli was one of my Harris hawks. I acquired him several years prior from a captive-breeding project and he assisted on a couple thousand of my lectures as well as on several national T.V. shows. During our appearances I would give a member of the audience a leather glove and have Stoli fly to them. He was fantastic around kids and had a personality more like a dog than a hawk.

Harris hawks are quite unusual raptors. Most raptors are very independent and solitary animals, Harris hawks are not. They are rather social and hunt in packs, like wolves.

It is thought that they evolved that way because their staple food supply is the black-tailed jackrabbit. A female jackrabbit can sometimes be larger than a Harris hawk. Perhaps they realize that hunting in packs proves to have a better success rate and it lowers the chance of injury from a rabbit's kick. They also perform an odd behavior called "back standing". This occurs when as many as three hawks perch on top of one another's shoulders like a totem pole.

Stoli was perched on my passenger seat's headrest. His bells jingled as I bounced over a series of potholes, making the truck's suspension handle like a "boot camper" running through tires. The bells are considered poor-mans telemetry. While he followed me through the forest I could listen to the bells to tell where he was instead of always looking around for him.

When we reached the top of the road, I parked on a snow pile and opened the passenger window. Stoli hopped from the headrest to the side view mirror, then sprung himself up to a tree branch that hung over the road.

When Stoli was a young chick I introduced him to windows. Most birds can not conceive the concept of windows or their own reflection. That is why so many birds fly into windows. They think the reflection is just another extension of the landscape and they perceive their refection as another bird. I once had a sparrow in my yard that beat himself against a mirror for days. I wonder if he ever understood why his opponent always looked as tired has he felt?

After letting Stoli closely observe windows, he became rather proficient at realizing whether a window was open or closed. He habitually flew in and out of my open bedroom window whenever he wanted to wander about the yard. He was also rather talented at flying in auditoriums and lecture halls.

It was bitterly cold and the snow squeaked beneath my feet as I walked into the woods towards the lake. I heard Stoli's bells ringing towards me as he gave me a close fly by, lightly nicking my left ear with his wing as he streaked past. That was one of his ongoing habits, especially when guests ventured along with us; he loved to test a stranger's nerves.

As he flew into the forest ahead of me, a half dozen squirrels froze to their branches, and grunted out warning calls to their colleagues. Stoli paid them no mind and continued to weave through the evergreens.

After I reached the edge of the lake, he landed on a branch directly over my head, which knocked a pinecone off the tree sending it to the snow below. As he jiggled his tail back and forth to straighten his feathers, he curiously turned his head upside down and peered down at the falling cone.

It was just after sunrise and a thick fog covered the lake. Some areas of the lake appeared to be solid ground as trees reached through the fog which covered the water like a soft carpet. The snow encircled the lake like a cotton ring; the open water appeared to steam like a cauldron when it met the warming sunrise air.

Stoli was getting restless and began hopping through the tree branches. To get his attention I picked up the fallen pinecone and tossed it up into the air. Stoli immediately dove out of the tree and caught it. He carried it to the ground and began swatting it with his feet. He then stomped on it and repeatedly gave it death squeezes until the dry cone fractured into tiny pieces.

This was one of the games we had played since he was first able to fly. Just like a tiger cub playing with its parents, it helps them develop into proficient hunters. It is their form of war games.

After making short work of the pinecone, he flew back up to a branch and began preening his feathers. I continued along the lake's edge and whistled for him to follow. He launched from his perch and languidly flew out over the water. A slight gust of wind began to clear the fog off the lake as it lifted Stoli up over my head, then lowered him down to skim his toes against the still water. He then lightly perched on a dead tree branch that stood in the middle of the lake. With a quick shake, he roused his feathers, then began to stand on one foot.

I lifted up my gloved fist and whistled. He leaped off the branch and swooped towards me. His bells made a "bubbly" whistle as they bounced over the surface of the water. At the very last second he pulled up on his "air brakes" gently landing on my fist.

He settled on my glove and I started walking further from shore toward a grove of pine trees. When I got to a small clearing I cast Stoli off my fist and he began to fly, and fly, and fly. As he disappeared from sight, so did the sound of his bells.

I whistled for him but he did not return. It was very unlike him; he never just flew off. I searched the surrounding area for him with no luck.

I then decided to drive up and down Poppletown Road to see if he might have been perched along the road-side. As I arrived at my truck, my eyes were searching the sky. It was not until I was about to start the truck that I realized Stoli was standing on the hood. His eyes peered in at me as if saying, "What took you so long?" I opened the window and he hopped inside. Then as if nothing happened, I pulled back onto the road and he took his regular seat.

This disappearing act soon became a habit. When

ever we went for a walk, he would vanish into thin air, always ending up on the hood of the truck. Then I realized why he did it. Harris hawks are designed for the warm American southwest; he hated the cold. Whenever it was too cold for him, he knew the heat from the truck's recently run engine would warm his feet.

It made me wonder, are animals more advanced than we believe? Do they have the ability to utilize other senses we have not even become aware of?

How did Stoli figure out to stand on the truck's hood to keep warm? When I flew him near my home, where the truck's engine was cold, he never stood on it. But this did not surprise me, it just added to my realization that animals know much more then they lead us to believe.

The Clarks nutcracker, a pigeon sized bird, show feats of insight that are literally super-human. It feeds on pine nuts throughout the winter. But where it lives, pine nuts are only in season for three weeks in September. So the nutcracker aggressively gathers pine nuts during those 3 weeks and buries them, sometimes traveling over ten miles between the trees and its storage sites. Throughout the three-weeks it will make a mental map of landmarks, such as broken trees and cliffs, just as we would remember a specific building or street corner. Using this map, it must remember the exact location of over 20,000 different underground storage sites, all within hundreds of square miles of the Grand Canyon. For the next 6 months, the nutcracker must solely rely on its mental map of the country side to find its food. It cannot remember by a visual map, because snow cover drastically changes the scenery. If it fails to remember its mental landmarks, the nutcracker will die through the winter. On average the Clarks Nutcracker finds over 90% of the 20,000 sites.

I once videotaped a lowland gorilla that waved at me, then stuck his tongue out like a spoiled child. Although he might have been mimicking what humans have done to him in the past, it still requires a rather complex thought process. Even humans develop by mimicking others; walk down any high school hallway to prove that.

I have watched a Chimpanzee obtain a banana suspended out of his reach by piling boxes on top of one another. When he realized the banana was still out of reach, he jumped off the boxes, broke off a tree branch of appropriate length. Then from the top of the boxes, he swung at the banana as if it were a baseball, knocked it down and ran off with it.

As I write this I have wild Mockingbirds nesting in my owl's flight chamber. The owl gives them no attention and the Mockingbirds seem fearless of him. As they feed their young, they come and go as they please through a tiny hole pulled open by growing vines. The Mockingbirds know that as long as the owl allows them to live there, they have the perfect security system against wild predators.

I have a pair of English Sparrows that made a nest in the clothes pin basket that hangs off my bathroom window. The entire nest is constructed from feathers dropped by my bald eagle, golden eagle, and Andean condor. None of these raptors gave a second thought to daring little birds that would sneak into their chambers for nesting material.

Also, I recently had a chipping sparrow build a nest next to my front porch. It was meticulously lined with a thick mattress of my German shepherd's hair.

For me, one of the most unexplainable and depressing displays of animal behavior took place one spring day after lecturing at the New York Botanical Gardens.

I arrived home from my presentation and opened the back of my truck to unload the animals. That afternoon I had a sixteen-foot python coiled on the front seat, and the back of the truck contained an alligator, a peregrine falcon, an Andean condor, and Stoli.

As I opened the condor's kennel to let him out, he began hissing at me and wildly swinging his head back and forth. He has never acted this way before. So I closed his kennel door, and began to unload the rest of the animals planning to see how he acted a few minutes from then.

I opened Stoli's kennel door and he was lying on his back, looking half-dead. I quickly reached in and pulled him out. I called out to my wife to start the car and drive us to the animal hospital. I wrapped Stoli in a blanket and laid him on the passenger seat. When I returned to the truck to quickly unload the rest of the animals, the condor was back to normal behavior again. I quickly walked him to his flight chamber and he acted fine.

It seemed that even though Stoli was in different kennel than the condor, and in no way could they see each other, the condor seemed to act as if he knew something was wrong. Not that he particularly cared for Stoli, but that a weakened animal was near. The condor never acted that way again.

As my wife and I rushed Stoli to my veterinarian, he appeared listless and shaky. Since he was unable to stand, I cradled him in my arms as my wife sped down the highway. About a mile from the hospital he did what I call the "final stretch." The final stretch is when a dying raptor hyper extends its head backward over its shoulders, as if its soul is traveling up its neck and out of the mouth. You may feel the heart softly beating and detect them breathing, but they are no longer there.

Although the hawk was unresponsive and functionally blind, the doctor desperately ran tests and administered first aid, but to no avail. Even the possibility of carbon monoxide poisoning was quickly ruled out. That can be immediately detected while drawing blood; a carbon monoxide victim's blood is always a bright cherry red.

After a mild seizure, Stoli fell limp in my arms. I held him for several minutes, before he was taken away for autopsy. I left the hospital with only his bells.

We never could find a solid reason for Stoli's death, I guess it was just his time. His bells have been inherited by a couple of his descendents and chimed through Mohonk Mountain House's Parlor while his nephew flew an engagement ring to my wife as I proposed to her.

But still, I cannot understand why my condor reacted to the situation the way he did. Being a top predator, could he in some way sense that death was near? For millions of years condors have fed off of the dead and dying; have they developed a paranormal knack for it?

Chapter VI

Over the Congo

Awakened by a burst of light, I felt the floor drop beneath me. I opened my eyes and focused on a glass of water hovering overhead. With the ice and liquid still within, it suddenly dropped splashing down on my chest. The ice slid down my shirt and cold water saturated my clothes. Gasping as if being thrown into a cold river, I tried to orient myself. With a crack in her voice, the flight attendant assured the passengers that this is normal activity, while whimpers and whines resonated from the seats behind me.

It was 3:00 a.m. and I was flying over the African Congo. Now over the equator we entered a violent thunderstorm. Heavy turbulence grabbed and shook the plane ferociously. Sitting next to me was an elderly South African woman holding rosary beads. The blinking light from the "fasten seatbelt" sign cut through the night reflecting off her lips as she silently prayed.

"Our father who, *Ah!*"

The plane dropped from under us and caught itself 500 feet below. Losing the ability to hold myself in the seat, I quickly snapped the seatbelt around my waist and clutched the armrests.

Twenty-two hours had passed since I rolled out of my bed in New York's Hudson Valley. Feeling slightly fatigued and cramped from airports and airline seats, pain began to well in my legs. To pass the time and discomfort, I placed my mind on the earth below: thinking, what *is Africa?*

Just as dogs hear sounds inaudible to humans, Africa's beauty is equally undetectable to the human senses. Her elegance overwhelms our narrow perception of beauty. More complex and unpredictable than any other region on the planet, Africa is still a dark mystery to the vast majority of Westerners.

When most people think of Africa they visualize pygmies, lions and Tarzan. However, in reality, pygmies have been all but extinct for decades, most Africans have never seen a lion and many Tarzan movies were filmed in India, even going as far as attaching cardboard cutouts to Asian elephant's ears in order for them to resemble their African relatives.

It is impossible for most to truly understand and respect Africa since they apply western standards to a land incomparable with any on earth. To appreciate Africa, one must understand the endless relationships between life, death, beauty, and brutality. Life cannot exist without death and its beauty can only be sustained through brutality.

Alone, Africa should be revered for its sheer size and "true" wealth: "true" wealth meaning natural and biological wealth. Only true wealth holds its value regardless of any economy or human created demand. Africa is four times larger than the United States; it contains twice as many people and spans seven time zones. It holds the greatest untapped natural resources in the world and farmlands capable of yielding 100 times more than produced today. If its present agricultural regions were utilized to their fullest, it could feed itself as well as all of Western Europe without clearing another acre. Africa has one-third the votes in the United Nations and may someday be the battlefield for the world's superpowers as the Middle East is today. Africa's diverse and abundant wildlife is unmatched anywhere on the planet. It is generally believed that human life first began on this continent. In the tree of life Africa is the root, supporting, anchoring and feeding the entire tree for some seven million years.

But to understand Africa as a whole one must see that within all its diversity, there is equal adversity. Africa's main problem seems to be the very things that make Africa so unique; cultural differences and linguistic boundaries.

More than six hundred and eighty million people make up about fifty nations in Africa. They are divided into over two thousand tribes and ethnic groups, most having their own specific language or dialect, making the unification of the entire continent impossible. For example, if this were the case in the United States, New York natives would speak an entirely different language than citizens of Connecticut. Just as well, New Jersey and Pennsylvania would also possess their own languages.

Thrown on top of this "continent of babble" is the end of colonialism and the growing pains of new government. Many countries found their white colonial masters were replaced with black neo-colonial leaders more concerned with individual power and wealth than their nation's development. One such is the former president of Gabon in western Africa: an undersized man who wore platform shoes and banned the word pygmy from his country's vocabulary. As his country lay at his feet starving and impoverished, he spent two million dollars on a house in Beverly Hills, California for his daughter and drove around in a gold plated Cadillac followed by a matching silver plated Cadillac ambulance.

Included in the equation is tribal allegiance. When a

president is elected, it is common or expected for him to fill all cabinet spots solely with members of his tribe or family. In most countries this would be considered unacceptable; in Africa it is just good political sense. One soon learns that nothing political in Africa stays unchanged for long. Just as a lion battles for rule over the pride, the laws of the jungle drain into the cities and towns in a constant struggle for political power. But Africa always seems to pick herself up, brush off the dust, and carry on.

What I witnessed in Africa reinforced the fact that the enormous majority of problems and complaints from my fellow U.S. citizens are nothing but the whines of a grossly spoiled child who does not get his own way and, above all, has no concept of reality. Compared to the seasoned African native, we are very soft and feeble.

Becoming entranced with the oscillating drone of the engines, I stared into darkness, while watching the red wing lights blink overtop the raindrops dancing outside my window and faded back to sleep.

The Twilight of the Wild

Chapter VII

The Graveyards of Hope

While driving out of Johannesburg, South Africa, I observed people standing along the roadside. As I sped past, I noticed that they were selling woodcarvings. Every mile or so I passed by groups of men selling small animal carvings along with huge wooden giraffes standing over five feet tall. Several of the artists took a more abstract approach by sculpting six-foot tall crane-like birds from car mufflers found along the road.

Set behind these salesman were small villages with "homes" made from metal sheets, cardboard, paper bags, and plastic. I use the word homes because none could be truly classified as a house. These villages are considered the "graveyards of hope".

The residents leave their native villages and migrate to the city seeking a better life. Unfortunately, the city does not have enough jobs to accommodate them upon their arrival. Penniless and hungry, they build these villages and wait for something better to come along. It seldom arrives. Most of these slums are illegal and the police, equipped with bulldozers, occasionally doze the village over. The very clever squatters make their homes from folded cardboard and sticks, disassembling them every morning. At the first rumble of a bulldozer, they grab their homes and run. Yet it never disrupts the Africans' will to survive because several days later the sun will rise over a newly constructed village built in its place.

Intrigued by these shantytowns, I decided to invite myself into the next one I discovered. About five minutes later I saw three dark human silhouettes standing on the horizon. Assuming they were near their village, I slowed down as I approached. Talking with them may give me an opportunity to enter their village as a new friend and not a strange intruder.

Throughout history the white man has brought many Africans turmoil and death, so I was extremely careful to respect their space and gain their trust before I imposed on their territory.

While pulling off to the side of the road, I gazed into a

small grassy valley sloping off to my right. At the bottom, about 20 feet below road level, was a small village no bigger than a football field.

I parked next to the three men and stepped out of the truck to greet them. Two of them smiled then looked toward the third man expecting him to be the spokesperson. Many of these villagers speak English but not to any great degree.

The tall man replied, "We fine boss, and you?"

After years of rule by the white minority, many South African blacks are still programmed to believe they are less than whites, or at least fake it in a white man's presence. I responded, "No need to call me boss, we are equal."

We all firmly shook hands and they told me their names. I could not understand what they said but I got the impression that they were all brothers. Immediately after the introductions, they proceeded to try and sell me anything that was not rooted to the earth or had the ability to run.

I would have loved to buy many of their creations but had over 10,000 more miles to travel and I did not want to carry anything that was not necessary.

Then I realized that if I purchased a carving, it might benefit us in two ways: One, it would help put food on their table, and two, they may be more inclined to allow me into their village. There were so many pieces to choose from- carved elephants, giraffes, baboons, and rhinos. Some were made from a dark glossy black wood, several were light tan with a wandering grain through them. I purchased a two-foot tall carved elephant for 60 Rand (about $20.00 U.S.) It was of museum quality made from light toned wood, showing a grain pattern that was a masterpiece in itself. Five-inch long tusks carved from cow bone protruded below its raised trunk.

While I paid for the carving, I heard a rumbling sound and then saw a beast of a truck abruptly pull up next to us skidding to a stop. It was a Land Rover, so new I looked for a colored chalk price tag on the window. The man driving shut the engine off and clumsily climbed out of the rig. A woman stepped out of the passenger door and the three brothers swarmed over to them to try for another sale.

As I browsed through the rest of their inventory, I noticed the man and woman seemed very arrogant and talked down to the natives. The man was of short build, pale, and significantly overweight. Having only a small handful of hairs matted to the back of his head, I would say he was legally bald. He was sweating profusely and his clothes seemed uncomfortably tight. His pants made an annoying whisping sound as he walked and when he laughed at his own crude remarks, his body gave a constricted jiggle while his straining, over-tight belt looked like a python making a kill. In addition, the belt gave his body the illusion that he was smuggling a motorcycle tire around his waist.

His lady friend was a tall, stunning, light skinned black woman with long braided hair and dramatically defined cheekbones. I have seen unmatched pairs like this throughout Africa.

Many of these beautiful women grow up penniless and will seek a wealthy man regardless of his looks or how he treats her. Beauty is skin deep but starvation is to the bone.

With a thick Dutch accent, the man began to bargain with the three brothers. He just drove up in a $60,000 vehicle, yet he was trying to haggle for the equivalent of two or three dollars. Unfortunately, this is a typical scenario in these parts. Knowing well these natives only make a few dollars a month, the Dutchman still convinced them to sell a carving for half its price. The brother's body language told me that they did not want to settle for such an unreasonably low price but they needed to feed their families.

Then the Dutchman really pushed his luck; he tempted the brothers with food. He showed them a can of chicken soup and tried to barter for more carvings. The man chose a babboon carving that would normally sell for 30 Rand. Even through a can of soup could never satisfy the hunger they feel everyday, they still considered the trade. It was almost a done deal until one of the brothers noticed a supermarket price tag still on the can; it read Price 5 Rand.

Suddenly, one of the brothers became outraged upon discovering he had almost been had. He began throwing his arms about, screaming in a mysterious language unknown to any of us, even to his brothers from the looks on their faces.

The couple became so terrified at this dramatic display of rage, the Dutchman quickly leaned over and dropped the carving in the dirt, and both he and his woman scampered back into their rig and sped off.

As the Land Rover faded in the distance, the three brothers burst out laughing, folding over, and holding their stomachs as they fell to the ground. With no care of getting dirty, they rolled on the earth laughing as the dust collected in the tears streaming down their faces. I suddenly became infected with the hilarity of the situation and the ground, too, drew me like a magnet. Before I knew it, I became part of this comical scene as if I was their long lost albino brother.

A few moments passed and we gained our composure and wiped the tears from our eyes. After I caught my breath, I decided to ask if I could visit their village. But as if they knew what I was about to ask, they invited me themselves. I helped them gather their carvings in old canvas bags and followed them towards the village. In broken English the tall brother says, "The secret to a happy life is to get at least one good laugh in a day." He could not be more true. Little would I guess that I would find one of the secrets to a happy life while rolling and laughing in a ditch along an African roadside.

I followed the brothers down a goat trail leading into the village. As they walked ahead of me, they continued to speak to me in an incomprehensible form of English.

I had a terrible time understanding them but could make out a few words and understood questions and statements by the pitch of their voices.

Half-listening, I began to absorb the dry desert-like environment. It was about 12:30 and the day was hot. At first the village seemed to be abandoned. No sounds or movements could be detected. I saw that the shelters were typical of most squatter villages I have visited; scrap wood, sheet metal, and plastic molded the architecture.

We walked into the village by squeezing between two metal shacks. I became slightly startled when I noticed that every home contained people. Sitting in the dark shadows to keep cool from the hot sun, they began to emerge from their boxes. As many as 10 people crawled out from each shelter of less than 15 feet by 15 feet. People appeared endlessly from everywhere and slowly walked toward us. As if I were an alien, the entire village gathered around me and stared. Many of the younger children had never seen a white man before and approached me with caution and curiosity.

An older man with a baritone voice said, "Good afternoon". Before I could respond, one of the brothers told everyone what he did to the fat Dutchman, and the group roared with laughter. Not really knowing what to say, I smiled nervously and said, "Hello" until the man with the baritone voice struck up a conversation with me.

"My name is Bakari, please relax and feel at home. We

don't have much but you are welcome to all of it."

Thanking him for his hospitality, I mentioned that I just stopped to take a rest from driving and I would be very grateful if he would show me around the village. He was delighted to do so. I noticed during our conversation that most of the villagers followed me around and stared, many with big smiles, some with unsure expressions. The children were simply puzzled.

Bakari began the tour with his home; it was made from three sheets of rusted metal with jagged sharp edges. I could see several white scars on his right shoulder that matched the burred metal edge of one wall; he must occasionally cut himself when he exited his home. His floor was nothing more than packed dirt with a mixture of canvas and plastic bags sewn into a bed mat and blanket. Next to the mat was a small jury-rigged cooking stove made from a rusted out bucket and a 6" by 6" piece of metal fence. In the corner opposite his bed mat was a bag that looked like it previously held grain or animal feed. It was modified with a drawstring cord and laid open exposing some of his more personal belongings, old faded pictures of his many wives and children, and various identification and tribal papers.

He then took me down a rough, muddy path scarred with hundreds of dried bare footprints. A thunderstorm the night before had flooded most of the low-lying areas. Hacked up slabs of wood bridged deep puddles of stagnant bacteria-ridden water where babies played together naked.

There was no electricity, running water or bathrooms. Towards the back end of the village, a small ditch was considered the bathroom for the whole community. I did my best to stay away from that area. It was rather easy because even if one could not see it, one would know it was there.

The older children ran through the paths kicking a homemade soccer ball constructed from plastic bags and string while wearing out-dated American clothes, most likely donated by a foreign church group.

Bakari continued the tour while six or seven villagers followed us like a celebrity entourage. Several children became rather comfortable with my presence and began to grab my pant legs and hold my hands.

Within one shelter, a large group of elderly natives sat perfectly still ignoring my presence. They only expended enough energy to occasionally swat flies away from their faces, until one elderly man turned his head and stared at me with his piercing cataract clouded eyes. His dark wrinkled face showed years of bitter anger, while his eyes expressed a distrust that I have never before seen in a human. He bitterly snapped a comment at me in his native tongue. As Bakari returned a scolding comment in my defense, I smiled the comment off and respectfully continued on.

"Bitterness and despair run deep in these slums," Bakari said, "Many minds are wasted here. Every soul in this walking cemetery could succeed in the modern world if given the respect, education and opportunity."

He pointed to a young girl several yards away. She is a cute child about twelve years old playing tag with her sisters, using an old goat as a shield. She circled around the animal keeping just out of reach.

"Her name is Shakir," Bakari said, "which means child born in the grace of God. Her family migrated from Nigeria in hope for work. Her mother brags all day how smart her daughter is. She says Shakir is always the smartest in the class, someday she will be a rich doctor and our whole family will live in a beautiful home by the city and have a big pool. Well, for two years now Shakir has not attended school because their family can not afford the annual tuition, the equivalent of twenty American dollars. Unfortunately, just like her nine older sisters she will most likely never go back to school, become one of a man's many wives and bear as many as five children before the age of twenty."

As we continued on, I got the impression that if this village were a single tribe, Bakari would be the cheif. He was clearly well respected and revered. Even the children were fond of him. He knew each one by name and it was obvious that he deeply cared for all of them.

One child yelled "Hey boss!" and kicked the soccer ball to me. Not realizing how much bounce a ball of plastic bags and string has, I booted the ball back to him, but it streaked over his head directly into a hedge of thorn bushes. The children yelped and chased after the ball. Two of the children had sticks and tried to beat the ball out of the bushes, only to knock it in further. With their efforts going nowhere, I walked over and carefully weaved my body between the thorny branches to retrieve their ball. The children yelled, "No, no, no, use de stick, use de stick, de snakes, de snakes!"

Snakes are a huge problem in these villages. When the village's garbage begins to pile up it attracts armies of rodents, and the rodents attract snakes, most of them poisonous. The black mamba, for example, can inject enough venom with a single bite to kill ten grown men. Ever since I was six years old, I loved and handled snakes so I was not concerned with the threat, but still remained cautious. While I attempted pulling the ball out of the brush, thin shreds of plastic bag snagged and hung from the needle-like thorns. I freed the ball after a couple firm tugs, then passed it to a child who began juggling it with his feet as well as any soccer pro.

"These tin shacks trap many talents and dreams," Bakari lamented. "Like caged lions, they wander in circles wearing down an endless path to nowhere."

The height of the sun off the horizon reminded me that precious travel time was being lost. I said this to Bakari and he offered to walk me back to my truck. We backtracked through the village and I said my goodbyes to the brothers. On the way a young boy who had silently hung onto the back of my shirt since I arrived here began tugging harder until I almost had to drag him.

I turned and smiled, "I have to go now."

As he shook his head no, his eyes begin to well with tears.

"You come back?" his squeaky voice asked.

"No, I am sorry, I can't." I replied.

"Why?" he whined.

"Because this is not my home."

"Can I come home with you?"

"I'm sorry you must stay here and help with the village."

Without a response, he just stared at me and began to cry. Each time a tear ran off his face, my heart sank lower. When we met, I was his only connection with the modern world and he felt a little closer to that world when I was near. I knelt down next to him and he hugged my neck. His bony little elbows dug into my shoulders and I asked him, "What is your name?"

"Atu."

"Well Atu, it's nice to meet you, my name is Rusty. I really must go now but I promise that when I return home I will send you a letter. I have many friends in the city, they will come out and give it to you. You have my word."

I then gave him the carved elephant I had purchased from the brothers and told him to sell it and buy some food. Bakari said he would see to it and then walked me back to the truck.

"What does the future hold for you?" I asked Bakari.

"Ahh, a rough road far too dusty to see where it leads my friend. My name means 'one who will succeed' so my day shall come if the gods wish it to be. Until then I will help my people and pray."

As I started up the truck, Bakari handed me a black carved rhino and said, "This is for you, I just finished it today, I hope it brings you luck." I thanked him for everything and promised I would keep in touch.

When I returned home I immediately wrote a letter to Bakari and Atu offering to pay for the children's school tuition. But unfortunately when my friend attempted to deliver the letter, he learned that their village was bulldozed and they were forced to relocate to an unknown area.

The Twilight of the Wild

Chapter VIII

Night in the Kalahari

The land cruiser launched into the air then bounced onto the sandy desert. My rear view mirror showed the paved street pulling away like the end of a rope vanishing behind my whirling trail of dust. Soon only sand and scrub brush could be seen in all directions. After spending several days in South Africa, I left the paved roads and trekked over the sand into southern Botswana's Kalahari Desert.

The trail was corrugated like a washboard forcing the truck to violently vibrate and veer side to side. As I drove further into the desert, the deep sand was like snow and made the truck more difficult to handle.

Without police, speed limits, or people for hundreds of miles, I felt free to drive as fast as I could. But the loose sand would eventually throw me out of control when I dared to push my luck.

This truly untamed part of Africa is endless rust-red sand dunes dotted with solitary trees and scattered grasses. The Kalahari Desert is a part of the largest continuous area of sand in the world. The area covers approximately 2.5 million square kilometers within the countries of Congo, Gabon, Angola, Democratic Republic of the Congo, Zambia, Zimbabwe, Botswana, Namibia, and South Africa, with some areas of sand reaching over 300 feet deep. Despite the fact that the Kalahari lacks any surface water, it is technically not a desert. It is a semi-arid zone, but none the less it is one of the most treacherous lands to travel. Yet, this rigorous climate has remained in constant balance supporting an overwhelming diversity of life for millions of years.

When I reached camp I pitched my two-man pup tent next to a dune and started a fire. While I cooked an ostrich steak over the flames, I watched the moon slowly peek up over the horizon.

Sitting hundreds of miles from modern civilization, I could hear the faint hum of silence. Given that our world is drowning in human created noise, silence is a quality of life countless people lack; many individuals have never experienced a single minute of pure silence, whether the faint hum of a refrigerator or the blast of a car, noise surrounds us.

As night approached an odd sound began to resonate from the bushes next to me.

Eee Eee Eee, Eee Eee Eee...

Soon the air was overwhelmed with the sound. I poked my flashlight into one of the bushes and learned that there were Gecko lizards, thousands of them calling from the bushes for a mate.

The gecko's love song became rather hypnotic as I lay on the ground and watched the stars. The sheer number of stars was overwhelming and the cooling air made them all intensely shimmer and pulsate. As gravity connected me to the lower hemisphere of the earth I felt as if I were peering down from the night sky gazing upon an infinitely huge city. To this day, never have I looked overhead and found stars more magnificent than in the Kalahari sky.

The bright moon illuminated an eerie glow over my surroundings and without the need of a flashlight, I clearly saw a black-backed jackal tiptoe past my tent in search of food. As her sensitive ears detected something under the soil, she leaped straight into the air and upon landing swiftly dug up a mouse which she promptly swallowed whole. Most jackals execute this unusual vertical leap as they locate prey; it is a rather comical habit to watch.

Weighing only about 20 pounds, the jackal resembles a small coyote. These nocturnal animals feed on small rodents, bugs, and occasionally, wild fruit.

I learned one morning that jackals are very inquisitive and mischievous after noticing my leather sandals were stolen during the night. The only clues left behind were jackal footprints leading into the desert, accompanied by the tracks of my sandals bouncing across the sand as they were dragged in its mouth. This seemed par for the course at the time since a human thief in Johannesburg two days prior stole my sneakers.

Fortunately, I was barefoot for only three days when a bushman noticed my need for footwear and traded me a pair of sandals for a toothbrush (unused of course), and a knife. The sandals were not exactly stylish, made from the tread of a blown out truck tire they sometimes seemed more uncomfortable than the hot sand, but I suppose they were better than nothing.

After the jackal gulped down the mouse she put her nose to the air and swiftly detected my presence. As she tilted her head and made eye contact with me, I realized I was most likely, the first human she had ever seen. After several seconds of interest, she tiptoed passed me with no appearance of concern and meandered out of sight over the dunes.

I turned my attention to the sky and realized the moon appeared to be shrinking. A half-hour before it was full, and now it was at half phase. It was a lunar eclipse.

As the earth's shadow gradually covered the moon, its last glowing sliver faded to black, and the desert was swallowed in absolute darkness. Seconds later a group of jackals began frantically yelping like dogs in a pound and then a spotted hyena began wailing over and over again.

whoop, whoop, whoop.

Spotted hyenas have over ten different vocalizations that can be linked with specific behaviors. If familiar with these sounds, one can imagine much of their actions without seeing them. For example when a spotted hyena "whines or whinnys" which is a series of loud, high pitched squeals and chattering noises, it is usually begging for food or was just weaned from its mother.

Like a squad of air raid sirens the rest of the pack chimed in like a frenzied gang of looters. Their sounds totally drowned out the tiny jackals and, as they ranted and squabbled, they painted a clear portrait of the fierce competition for survival in the Kalahari.

The accelerated speed of the whoops lead me to believe the hyenas were challenging a lion over a kill. More than likely, a lion took advantage of the eclipse's complete darkness and tackled down an antelope.

The Kalahari lion with its characteristic black mane was once thought to be a subspecies of its own, but is now classified as a lion particularly well adapted to a desert-like environment. Its fur is lighter than lions elsewhere and serves as excellent camouflage in the sand.

They have also adapted the ability to go weeks without drinking water and survive on a minimal amount of prey. In this vast region, they must fight harder for their food than in any other territory because stalking is more difficult in such a wide-open area.

As I suspected, a lion's deep roar cut through the night and immediately the hyena whoops were replaced with high cackling laughs. This comedic, yet sinister sound which is associated with the common name "laughing hyena" is typically made by individuals while being chased or attacked. The lion must have been protecting her kill as the hyenas tried to steal it from her. I specify "her" because after a lion's typical twenty-hour day of resting, 90% of the time it is the female that hunts. Males simply trail behind the female until after the quarry is killed and then he will run up and claim "the lion's share".

With two deep bursts from the lion's lungs she called the rest of her pride.

AAAAAHHHHOOOO!,

AAAAAHHHHOOOO!

The chilling sound took my breath away. The rest of the pride must have arrived rather quickly because the hyenas began to whoop again. But now the sound had a slow drawn-out "o-o-o-o" which means the competition for the kill had become too fierce and the hyenas decided to hang back at a safe distance and wait for the lions to finish eating. Occasional fast whooping followed, which expressed their impatience while sitting on the side lines.

Night in the Kalahari

The moon then gradually reappeared brightening the desert once again, and I retired to my tent. As I fell asleep, I heard the hyenas bickering over the scraps from the kill, and the sound of lions calling to one another soon faded off into the night.

Chapter IX

The Wateringhole

While my wife Melissa and I were honeymooning in Zimbabwe, we agreed to spend our last day in Africa watching the sun set over a small watering hole we had found the day earlier.

Arriving two hours before dark we parked thirty-yards from the water's edge. I threw a soft blanket on the hood of the truck and we lay on top of it. The hot sun massaged our shoulders as it fell behind us and the cooling late afternoon breeze blew through a neighboring acacia tree making its thin branches shiver.

After opening a bottle of South African wine, we lightly tapped our glasses together to toast our last day in Africa as newlyweds. Then we leaned back against the truck's windshield and stared silently upon the watering hole.

It was no larger than a soccer field and aside from several wildebeest grazing in the background, it seemed empty of life. Its flat shoreline and the stillness of the water gave the illusion it was a giant mirror that had fallen from the sky, and the wind blown sand had concealed its straight edges.

Soon life began to emerge all around us. A pair of Egyptian geese flew in from the north and landed in front of the truck. Each slowly waded into the pool until the water began to carry their buoyant bodies towards the middle. While dipping their heads into the water and preening their feathers, they slowly floated about.

Our attention was drawn to a splashing sound off to our right. It was an elderly male baboon smacking the surface of the water with his hand. A troop of 30 more arrived after him in a loose pack like a tribe of prehistoric humans.

Reminding Melissa and me of modern man at a public beach, they all separated into groups or "cliques", claiming their own spot next to the water's edge. The larger groups contained entire families with overactive babies wearing down the patience of their parents. The smaller groups were adolescents. They groomed each other like teenage girls and seem to be the "show offs" of the troop. Several older baboons were more of the "swinging single" type. They wandered up and down the beachside trying to impress the opposite sex while occasionally taking a wild punch at a rival to prove their dominance.

The baby baboons began to wander away from their parents and wildly look for trouble. There were twelve infants, some clinging upside down to their mother's chest and were small enough to fit in the palm of one's hand.

Although small, the young displayed amazing feats of strength. They would wrestle, play tag and even lift giant balls of dried elephant dung over their heads before hurling it at their playmates like a dodge ball. Soon after, their mothers would try and calm them down with a gentle yank on the tail while the elderly adults sat stone-faced like old disapproving school principals.

It is fascinating how human-like baboons behave. When watching them one can see the raw basics of human behavior that has formed us all. The first wild baboon I had ever encountered was scaling a fence in Botswana. Until I approached for a closer look, I was convinced it was a small human. I will always remember the eerie feeling I got as I approached to greet him. Our eyes met and he proved me wrong.

Suddenly, the baboons began to get restless and several of the large adults made a loud barking sound. Immediately the entire troop backed away from the water and the parents gathered their young. While using their tail for a kickstand they all stood on their hind legs and stared towards the water.

Melissa and I tried to see what the concern was, but

the sun's reflection off the water hid what was there. Then about 20 feet off shore the water started to churn. As the troop began to wrangle their young, they barked louder and louder. The surface began to settle when a long dark figure slowly began to appear through it. Two eyes bulged out of the water like a submarine's periscope, a crocodile.

Just as quickly as it appeared, it slipped back beneath the water and the baboons began to settle down, but stayed a safe distance from the water. Then one of the large adults climbed 40 feet up a dead tree and sat out on a branch all by himself. As if sitting in a lifeguard tower, he became the lookout for the entire troop, gazing from under his prominent brow surveying the land for predators.

While this was taking place, the Egyptian geese high-tailed it back to shore and were nervously honking as they paced back and forth.

I pointed out a ripple in the water and Melissa immediately focused her video camera on it. Like a fisherman's lure being reeled in, a thin split in the water rolled towards the shore as the ridge of the crocodile's head barely peeked over the surface.

Slowly its head emerged from the dark water and it gently slid its body over the mud. The crocodile lifted her twelve-foot long, 500-pound body off the ground, and lumbered up to dry land. Its belly was distended, and hung to the ground swinging side to side proving to be void of food.

Unexpectedly, a second crocodile crawled from the water, which startled the geese into flying directly over us towards the sun. This crocodile was slightly larger than the other, but had an equally empty stomach. He flopped down directly next to the other, and like flipping a switch from animated to inert, they both lay on the sand as still as statues.

"Look!" Melissa said with a thrilled whisper. She pointed towards the horizon at a herd of elephants. From around a grove of trees, they slowly banked a turn like a tight flock of birds and began steamrolling towards us.

The grazing wildebeests indignantly removed themselves from the elephant's path without ever raising their heads from the grass. As the elephants gained excitement from the smell of the water, they also gained speed. The herd's matriarch galloped to a stop at the edge of the watering hole and all thirty of her followers lined up their broad "couch pillow" feet next to her, unrolling their trunks to drink.

An elephant essentially walks on its tiptoes atop tough and fatty "shock absorber" soles that help the elephant carry its heavy weight and move silently.

This was a maternity herd, consisting entirely of females and their young. The matriarch that boldly led this herd was a towering nine feet tall and weighed over 9,000 pounds. Her long tusks and sunken temples showed her age, she must have been over 50 years old. The dark scars carved along her tusks told her life story like a totem pole.

Her herd was one of the very few that has survived the poaching era. The majority of Africa's elephants have been killed for their ivory tusks.

Each elephant inhaled over ten gallons of water at a time, then sprayed it into its mouth like a fire hose. Some babies were only three-foot high and always stood beneath their mothers or relatives. Although still nursing, the tiny ones tried to vacuum up small handfuls of water with their trunks, but the water always seemed to spill out before it reached their mouth. One newborn elephant finally gave up and stuck its whole face under water to see if he would have better luck. Melissa had trouble aiming the video camera because the sight of them made her cry.

After getting their fill of water, they proceeded to lean to their sides and fall into the wateringhole. As they bathed, the adults trumpeted and sprayed water into the air, while they rolled a thick coat of mud over their skin. When all were covered in mud, they rose to their feet and gathered back into a tight formation. After communicating with a series of low-pitched grumbles, they made sure their young were guarded on all sides. Then the giant matriarch trumpeted, and they all marched behind her across the savanna.

Elephants communicate with low-pitched grumbles. Most of their sounds are infrasonic and cannot be detected by humans. An infrasonic elephant call might carry over an area of about thirty square kilometers; its range is even greater at night.

One day while interacting with three captive African

elephants, I detected the sound of their infrasonic call for the first time. I did not hear it; I felt it. As the three ten-foot tall elephants stood within arms reach, they inspected me with their trunks, then suddenly stood perfectly still. As I saw the skin on the front of their heads slightly flutter, an invisible force began vibrating my insides. Although unable to hear their calls, they were powerful enough to be felt.

As the herd moved away, night began to fall. In the distance we could see their dim silhouettes throwing trunk fulls of sand over their backs, as their young weaved between their legs as if playing amongst a forest of trees. Like being squeezed by an invisible lasso, the entire herd drew close together, then headed into the darkness.

With night gradually overtaking the wateringhole, the baboons raced around it like a stage crew closing a show. They all dipped their lips into the water and enjoyed a "nightcap" and filed into the bush to climb into the trees for the night. The stirred up water settled like a mirror again and the crocodiles switched back to "animate" mode, sliding their bodies back beneath the dark water. Then along with the rustling sound of baboons settling in the trees, the day ended.

On our drive back to camp I told Melissa how the whole experience reminded me of a theater production. Center stage was the wateringhole, the baboons were the stage crew, the geese were the warm up act, and the elephants were the headliners. The crocodiles were security, they cleared the stage for the main act, and then returned to duty after the show just as the great "Production Manager" above shut off the lights.

But the more I thought, the more I realized that the darkness not only concluded the performance; it began another one: this one starred two hungry crocodiles.

Chapter X

The Lounge

I stopped my truck as the street light turned from yellow to red and a mass of uniformed school children playfully teased each other as they crossed the street in front of me. The streets were crammed with people en-route to their favorite places to shed the stress of the work week. It was a Friday night in Bulawayo, the second largest city in Zimbabwe. The name means the "place of slaughter" due to its bloodstained past during a slow transition into a modern city.

I headed for a private bush lounge on the outskirts of the city. This bush lounge is much like an oasis in the desert. Seemingly in the middle of nowhere, it is a well hidden, high-class cocktail lounge and meeting place for the wealthier locals and well-to-do "wanna-be" safari travelers. I use the term "wanna-be" for the reason that most of these travelers would not consider a safari if it did not include an African servant serving them an eight-course dinner every night.

The thatched roofed lodge was set within a group of large acacia trees which effortlessly held in the air a weaver finch nest that weighed over a thousand pounds and was the size of a small truck. The nest hummed like a giant beehive as hundreds of finches zipped in and out while feeding their chicks.

Vervet monkeys casually strolled out of the bushes and begged for handouts as I got out of the truck. I noticed that if one did not give them any food, they would sit on his vehicle until he returned. The monkeys were rather chunky, so I believe their methods worked well for them.

I walked into the cocktail lounge which was finished in dark mahogany with brass adornments, and decorated with large vases of creeping ivy. The bar was equal in quality to any New York City establishment and an African bartender stood behind the bar displaying perfect posture in a white uniform and gloves. Hanging from the lizard-inhabited ceiling spun a shiny brass fan that was powered by a small waterfall which flowed outside the lounge.

In the far corner sat a group of white South Afrikaans. Their table was littered with empty wine bottles and cigar butts while they continually filled each other's glasses and loudly bantered back and forth.

At the bar sat five black Africans. They quietly spoke to one another with slightly slouched postures, evidence of a hard day of labor, and really seemed to enjoy each other's company. Feeling a welcoming energy from the men at the bar, I decided to sit by them.

As I approached, one of the men pulled out a bar stool. "Have a seat." he said in broken English. As I sat down, I motioned to the bartender that I would buy a round of drinks for the gentlemen and each of the men individually shook my hand in thanks.

One of the men who was very well spoken said, "Good evening, my name is Mothusi (Mo-tu-cee), are you a local?"

"No sir, I am from the United States. I stopped off here for the night before driving into the bush," I responded.

"To do what?" he replied with concern.

As I began to explain my reasons and intentions, the rest of the men leaned in to listen. After I concluded, they all seemed rather pleased. They were impressed with the fact that I was a single, independent person looking to observe and live their world first hand, not as a diamond investor, tourism company representative or scientist, but as an equal.

They told me that many Westerners have an awful habit of coming to Africa to exploit the people and its wildlife for personal gain, to even study the citizens as if they were wild animals. They seemed to believe that, no different than the cockroach, many Westerners infest all corners of the globe with the intent to take over and spoil the wealth of its inhabitants strictly for their own profit.

Relieved they approved of my presence, I asked if they were from Zimbabwe. "No" they all replied. One was from Botswana, two were from Nigeria and the two sitting at the end of the bar were brothers from Rwanda. They emigrated from their native homes to seek better work and became friends on the job. They were masons and showed a deep pride for their craft.

They agreed they have a better life here in Zimbabwe and are glad they moved from their homelands.

"Especially for Mawaka and Salongo" Mothusi said, indicating the two brothers from Rwanda sitting at the end of the bar. Mothusi told me they have lived a challenging life; the others nodded their heads in agreement.

Africans rarely complain or feel sorry for themselves, and are very respectful of what the fates bring them. So it did not surprise me when the brothers remained rather quiet while Mothusi explained their story.

Mothusi said softly, "Rwanda contains a lush jungle climate that provides home to three species of gorilla. Two of the three are true gorillas: the mountain gorilla and the lowland gorilla. These strikingly human-like animals live a peaceful sociable life in two separate areas in the Zaire River basin. Standing six feet tall, weighing up to six hundred pounds and having the strength of over ten men, our jungle ancestral remnants do not breed the terror and fear created by the third and most deadly species of gorilla. This species, commonly spelled g-u-e-r-i-l-l-a, is a strikingly inhuman, cold-blooded murderer. Killing without remorse, these socially deformed monsters appear as humans, and brutally murder innocent men, women and children as swiftly as they kill their worst enemies."

"Leftovers from the Hutu extremist government, they were responsible for murdering over five hundred thousand people during a three month period in 1994. The victims' only offense was belonging to the wrong tribe. Wherever they were killed, was where they were left to rot."

"No human, no less a child, should have to live like that!" his voice gains volume and passion as he stood up from his stool. "The outside world didn't seem to care, and many Rwandans seemed thrown aside, particularly by the United States."

He continued, "When Hussein invaded Kuwait in 1990, the U.S. was first in line to right the wrongs. Yet, four years later, Rwandan's nightmare seemed to be overlooked. Why? Because of the "black blood" known as oil! Which is as valuable to Americans as their green money! Is the 'black blood' worth more than the blood of blacks?"

As he sat back on his stool he said, "Even when the genocide was halted after the Tutsi rebels took power in July 1994, the land is still plagued by fighting, and stinks of death."

"In this day and age when the rest of the world knowingly allows acts like this to take place, we are no more civilized than we were five thousand years ago." While pointing at the two brothers, Mothusi continued, "The two boys that sit in front you had to hide, fight, and watch their family be killed right before their eyes!" Lifting his beer he adds, "In any other country, they would not even be old enough to drink this beer. Yet, in Rwanda they have lived the lives of a thousand men. It's simply not right!"

Speechless, I had no response. Words could not give justice to the moment. Then, just like a channel being turned on a television, they switched to their everyday humor and conversation as if nothing had happened. They welcomed me into their group and we spent several hours leaning on the bar, discussing our two very different worlds.

While discussing the subject of popular music, one of the brothers made a comment that will always stick in my mind. He said, "In 1994 when the rest of the world's children listened to rap music, my brother and I would hide underneath the floor boards listening to the screams of our family and neighbors being pulled from their beds in the middle of the night to be murdered in the streets. That was the only sound we heard at night. Even the wild animals no longer squabbled over meals during the night because they leisurely feasted on our dead and became fat and lazy."

Chapter XI

Mosi-oa-Tunya
The Smoke that Thunders

As we drove up over a tiny hill, Melissa and I noticed a huge cloud of misty white smoke rising up from the horizon. Unlike typical smoke which appears to rise up through the air and thin into the sky, this smoke seemed to ride on the air, then eventually settle back towards the earth.

We traveled about ten miles closer when the smoke

began to sparkle like a rainbow. Spectrums of color gradually appeared and faded while bright pinpoints of light pulsed like a thousand beacons. The sight of this shimmering cloud was so captivating that we did not realize a 10,000 lb. elephant was crossing the road directly in front of us.

I slammed on the breaks, screeching the truck to a halt. The startled elephant spun his body around to face us. He spread his ears out to the sides of his head displaying his enormous size. Then he loudly trumpeted as he swung his trunk back and forth in rage. Threatened by our sudden appearance, he assumed this defensive posture to frighten us away.

Despite Melissa's frightened pleas to back away from the elephant, I held our ground by remaining where we had stopped. After several quick flaps of his ears, the elephant stepped towards the truck and held his head high above his ten-foot tall shoulders. Then he stared down at us over his gigantic six-foot long tusks; each tusk must have weighed over 150lbs.

I noticed the elephant was "right-handed", because his right tusk was more worn down than his left one, which meant he used that one more often. Unfortunately, that was the one almost knocking on our windshield.

The elephant then raised his trunk into the air, and began sniffing our vehicle. An elephant's trunk contains nearly 150,000 muscles and nerves, providing it with extreme flexibility and sensitivity. Lacking any bones, the trunk is equipped with two finger-like points on the end. An African elephant can pick up fruit the size of a marble as well as break a 12-inch thick branch off of a tree. This elongated proboscis provides a means for smelling, breathing, touching, drinking, and eating. During the dry season, when water is low, an elephant will dig holes and use its trunk to tap underground springs. The trunk also acts as a hose, whether for a drink or a dust bath. A coating of dust or mud on the skin repels sun and insects.

In the past, many people would unearth an elephant's skull and think it was the skull of a Cyclops; the hole to facilitate the elephant's trunk was mistaken for an eye socket.

When the elephant's trunk began to gently investigate our vehicle as if it had a mind of its own, I began to slowly creep forward to show a mild aggression. This is something that needs to be done to an overzealous animal that has the ability to tip your truck over. As I slowly inched forward, the elephant spread his ears out and took a charging posture. This massive wall of muscle standing six-feet taller than the hood of our truck was the ultimate form of intimidation. From ear to ear he was wider than the truck. As he stared down at us, his tusks were inches from our windshield, and the heavy breathing from his trunk fogged our glass.

As the largest land animal on earth, one would believe its enormous size carries an equal sense of confidence, but it does not. When most elephants threaten a human with a charge, they are bluffing, especially the males. When encountering male elephants while on foot in the bush, one can usually ward off a charge with a fair amount of yelling and waving of the arms. Believe it or not, sometimes simply throwing a small stick at an aggressive elephant will send them running in the opposite direction. Not that throwing a stick could ever hurt an elephant, it is much like throwing a pencil at a human. But the mere action of a measly human throwing something at them is enough to confuse them and discourage further aggression. But, the case can be much different when encountering a female elephant, especially with young. Do not try the stick throwing approach with a mother elephant. She might chase you down with the stick you have just thrown, and "jam it where the sun doesn't shine." As with most animals, including humans, mothers protecting their young can become very unpredictable and aggressive. But, when you think about it, they are the most predictable: you know they will kill you. How can you tell the difference between a male and female elephant? Let's just say that when you see a male elephant, "it" is quite obvious.

While we continued inching towards the elephant he began to back away. Then with an amazing amount of grace and speed, he lumbered off the side of the road and into the bush.

We lingered in the area for a few minutes, watching him pull off trunkfuls of dried thorny leaves and stuff them into his mouth. Occasionally he would turn his head in our direction and give an aggressive earflap and headshake, just to let us know he did not forget we were there. Then after he slowly disappeared into the thick brush, we continued on our way towards the shimmering cloud.

About one-half mile past the elephant, we pulled the truck off to the side of the road and followed a thin path on foot. As my feet touched the African soil, a dust cloud lifted into the hot dry air. The sun baked ground emitted heat like an electric stove, causing hundreds of tiny lizards to dart around the ground, panting like dogs while searching for the tiniest shadows of shade. The surrounding land was parched, the sparse clumps of bristly dry grass crackled beneath our feet, and the larger surrounding vegetation seemed to pout from thirst.

We followed this thin sandy path as it meandered through the barren grass. It led towards a patch of dense jungle which seemed to "carry" the shimmering cloud. We started to hear a faint rumbling sound in the distance and it became louder and louder as we approached the jungle. Soon all we heard was a constant thundering roar.

Then within a matter of a single footstep, we entered a lush jungle. The change in our surroundings was so extreme, that at one moment as I stood on the path, my left foot touched bone dry sand and scrub brush, while my right foot was stepping within a lush rainforest. It was as if we were standing on a page in a photo album and walked from one photograph to another.

Green broad leaf vegetation grew towards the sky, so tightly interwoven with each other, that it seemed as if a giant could run by and pick up the entire rainforest like a basket.

A cool mist continuously fell from the sky and the fallen water would collect in the forks of trees like tiny ponds. Around these miniature watering holes, small multi-colored birds gathered to drink, bathe, and preen their feathers. The birds sparkled within this micro-jungle, as the sun reflected off the mist that collected on their feathers.

Suddenly a three-foot tall monkey jumped out of a tree and landed directly in front of us. He sat on his hindquarters and stared at us with deep curiosity, almost as if he was trying to communicate with his mind. He then turned around and began to walk down the path. As if acting as a tour guide, he walked in front of us and occasionally would turn around to see if we were following. The image of this monkey walking us down the path was priceless.

Soon the monkey, along with us, became soaking wet from the mist and the rumbling noise became so overwhelmingly loud, Melissa and I had to communicate by screaming to one another. As we made our way through the showering mist, the jungle opened up in front of us. The monkey lazily hopped up to a branch and looked back towards us as we followed behind him. Then as we walked up next to him, the roaring sound rattled our ribs.

Through a thick cloud of churning mist, roared one of the seven natural wonders of the world, Victoria Falls, the largest curtain of water on the earth. The Kololo tribe living in Zimbabwe during the 1800's named Victoria Falls, Mosi-oa-Tunya - The Smoke that Thunders.

At a mile wide, the Zambezi River fuels Victoria Falls. Suddenly, this calm, glass-like river violently transforms as sixteen hundred million cubic feet of water per second (yes, per second), plunges 300-feet creating continuous explosions of water in the pool below. It vibrates your skin, shaking your soul.

In every direction, rainbows faded in and out. Blowing mist filled our eyes with water and soaked our clothes, while a hurricane of rising spray exploded hundreds of feet into the air, capturing the attention of anyone within a 25-mile radius.

The Zambezi is the fourth longest river in Africa and is one thousand, six hundred and fifty miles long. It flows through eastern Angola, western Zambia, forms the border of northeastern Botswana, and separates Zambia and Zimbabwe. It then crosses central Mozambique where it branches out into the Mozambique Channel.

I had a great dilemma in writing about Victoria Falls. The human mind is too limited to accurately translate such drama and beauty. A language that could fully describe what your eyes see, does not exist. Words cheapen the vision.

Gazing at Victoria Falls is hypnotic. Her explosive roar deafens all conversations forcing one to silently stare at her, inhale her mist, and absorb her beauty. She demands all of your attention, and you are more than willing to give it to her.

Within seconds, Victoria Fall's image, power, and beauty, creates a passion within one's soul that would take years to develop between two people. When you leave "Victoria", you feel as if you are forever walking away from a soul mate. You leave wanting to take her home with you. It is a desire you will always feel, but never fulfill. There are no words to describe this "Queen" that would do her justice, and I will not try.

Melissa and I held hands and stared for as long as we could. We began to lose track of time, so we reluctantly pried ourselves away from "Victoria", and walked along her edge toward the Zambian border.

As I passed our monkey friend I said to him, "Come on, let's go to Zambia." The monkey looked at me with a slightly tilted head, his hair clumped together from the falling mist, making him look like a punk rocker. Then he slicked back his hair with both hands, which made him look like a 1950's greaser.

As he continued to slick back his "do," Melissa and I walked along a cliff hanging path on the edge of the falls, but the monkey never followed. I am sure he believes there is no better place for him to be, than where he is. He is right.

After a short walk, we passed through a small border post of custom agents ready to inspect our immigration documents. After they stamped our passports, we walked into Zambia.

From this location, one must enter Zambia via an old iron railroad bridge. The Victoria Falls railroad bridge was completed in 1905, and it quickly became a vital trade route between the two countries as well as hosting many clandestine operations during times of political turmoil. The bridge helped kick start Victoria Fall's tourist trade which has grown year after year. Not only was it a vital trade route, it is currently a tourist attraction. The bridge is home to the highest commercial bungee jump in the world. For roughly 100 U.S. dollars, one can bungee jump 350-feet off the bridge, over the Zambezi River. I never had the desire to pay money in order to jump off a perfectly sturdy bridge, so we continued on into Zambia.

While looking deep into the gorge of the Zambezi, I realized that if the bungee cord ever broke, the hippos and crocodiles would have a field day. I am sure that from years of watching people "fall" off the bridge, then miraculously spring back into the air just before hitting that water, has the hippos and crocs gathering below the bridge in hopes of a "technical failure". After leaping, the bungee jumpers are lowered into a small boat and brought to shore. Then, they must scale a craggy cliff to get back onto flat land, making "recovery" seem more treacherous than the leap.

Melissa and I walked along the railroad bridge into Zambia where we met four young native boys caring five-gallon spackle buckets full of flavored ice.

"Hey boss, would you like some ice?" one on the Zambians asked.

"Lets see what you have" Melissa replied.

Immediately each of the boys sat on the railroad track and pried the tops off their buckets while holding them between their knees. After a fair amount of effort, they popped their lids and displayed their inventory. Each of their buckets were meagerly filled with half-frozen bricks of juice, all floating in a smorgasbord of previously melted flavors. The spackle that the bucket originally held would have been more appetizing, but Melissa and I both purchased a block of ice to acknowledge their proprietary efforts.

As we departed company with the boys, one of them said, "Thank you sir, my name is Osborne, if you ever need ice in the future, please look for me."

"I will Osborne, and you guys keep up the good work." I replied while we began to walk down the tracks in separate directions.

After taking a rather uneventful stroll along the Zambian border, we walked back to our truck in Zimbabwe. We then decided to drive into the city of Victoria Falls.

Victoria Falls has turned into a "tourist town". Twenty years ago Victoria Falls had just less than 100 permanent European residents. Now the streets are filled with Europeans, as well as souvenir shops, tour guides, and street merchants.

As we drove into town, I almost forgot we were in Africa. The city seemed no different than any American vacation town. Being one of the most popular tourist attractions in the world, provides many opportunities for the few people within the tourist industry. But it does not provide solutions for much of Zimbabwe's social problems.

In Victoria Falls, as well as all of Zimbabwe, poverty is an extreme problem. Minutes after we parked our car along the roadside, groups of sickly people swarmed around us begging for food or money.

This is always a difficult situation to face, especially when the children are begging. We had enough money in our pockets for them to retire on. But if you are seen freely handing out money to strangers, you can get into serious trouble. Particularly when you run out of money to give.

In situations like this, we keep an eye on the individuals in need while we are in their vicinity, then when we are ready to leave, we discreetly pass them what money and food we can spare, then quickly move on.

In addition to a lifetime of poverty, Zimbabwe's involvement with the war in the Democratic Republic of the Congo, drained hundreds of millions of dollars from the economy. The average income in Zimbabwe is under $1,000 dollars a year. But that "average" is not average. There are few middle-class citizens in Zimbabwe. It seems that the citizens of Zimbabwe either have it all, or have nothing.

Unfortunately, AIDS is steadily weakening Zimbabwe's already crippled economy. Having the highest rate of AIDS infection in the world, one out of every four adults in Zimbabwe is afflicted with the virus that causes AIDS. Two thousand five hundred Zimbabweans a week die from the disease and that figure is expected to rise rapidly in the coming decade. It is predicted that in several years AIDS will not be Zimbabwe's only major problem; they will also have a severe orphan epidemic. Currently one out of every five Zimbabwe children has lost at least one of their parents to AIDS.

As the people gathered around us, I firmly made it clear to the adult beggars, that they were not getting anything. It is healthy to sometimes put up a "tough" front to the overzealous adult beggars; otherwise they can become very pushy and demanding.

When I started speaking with the children, the adults wandered off to look for other income opportunities. The specific attitude of adult beggars can shed light on why they are begging. The gentle polite beggar, generally has suffered much hardship and is making the best of their depressing situation. The beggars that act pushy and demanding are more often people too lazy to get a job and would much rather beg than work. But these rules do not hold true for the children, pushy or not, they are alone, scared, and fighting for their lives everyday.

Melissa and I started talking to a girl and her two younger sisters. All three of them looked like little neglected rag dolls; their tattered oversized clothing barely hanging on to them. Melissa asked their names and the oldest girl replied, "My name is Kambo. These are my sisters Mudiwa and Chipo".

"Why do you need money, does your mom and dad work?" I politely asked

"No sir, they can't work, my mommy and daddy died."

"I am sorry to hear that. When did they die?"

Her little face grew sadly depressed as she replied, "My daddy died two years ago, and my mommy died last year."

"How old are you?"

"I think I am nine", and after a long pause she added, "Mudiwa is seven, no six, and Chipo is five, I think."

"When are your birthdays?"

"I don't know."

"None of you know you birthdays?"

"No"

"Once I remember my mommy saying that Chipo was born in the summertime but I am not sure when."

"Who takes care of you and your sisters?" Melissa asked.

"I do." She proudly replied with a smile.

"Where do you live?"

"Anyplace we can sleep, where no one will bother us."

"Do people bother you a lot?" I asked with great concern.

"Yes, all the time. But it is always bad people that bother us; most nice people never pay attention to us."

"Why do the bad people bother you?"

"They try to take our food, blankets, and sometimes try to hurt us."

"Sometimes if I scream, they will run away."

It is sad to think that their only perception of "nice people" are the people that ignore them.

"You and your two sisters have been living on the streets all alone for the past year?"

"Yes, sometimes when it gets so cold at night, we hug each other to keep warm."

"Do you have any family, grandparents, uncles, aunts."

"No, they all have died."

I wanted to ask how their entire family died. I assume most of them died from AIDS, and the grandparents from old age. The average life expectancy in Zimbabwe is only 37 years old. But I noticed by the looks on their faces, that talking about their parents was too painful for them, so I never asked.

"Our family is the three of us." Mudiwa said.

"You are the three musketeers." I replied with a smile. And they all politely replied "Yes," not quite sure what I was talking about.

I then told them that Melissa and I were going to take a look around town, but we would like to see them before we leave."

"We will be around," she promised with a bright smile.

I think she was surprised that we were giving them so much attention. "Then we shall see you soon," I stated and lightly patted the three of them on the tops of their frizzy heads. As we walked away, they crossed the street and then tightly tucked into a dark alleyway to keep out of the sun.

Needless to say our stroll through the city of Victoria Falls was rather depressing. It is a vacationer's paradise, but it can be a resident's hell. Hidden within Victoria Fall's overwhelming beauty, the harsh realities of life continue to exist. Every night these lonely discarded children tuck themselves into the dark and dingy alleyways of this beautiful city, only to wake up the following morning, alone and hungry, like the unnoticed pebbles lodged in the grooves of a Ferrari's gas pedal.

While exploring ultra-modern storefronts and tourists arriving in their luxury cars, Melissa and I talked about the girls' situation. I have to admit our first thought was to scoop them up and take them home with us. But when reality set in we agreed to give them money, just to make their coming days a bit easier to handle.

We devised a plan to safely get the money to them. When giving children in this position money, it is not safe to hand it to them in view of adults in their same position. Unfortunately, there are some people in this world that are just "mean;" if they see a child with money, they will steal it, and perhaps do far worse to the child. Predators live among the civilized as well as the wild.

Our plan would keep them safe from that possibility, at least until they got the money, then it would be up to them to hide it. We had to convince ourselves that our new little friends gained enough "street smarts" during the year they have been homeless and alone.

In Victoria Falls there is an old locomotive "parked" as a monument in what seems to be the "village square." I placed a generous amount of money in a brown paper bag, crumpled it up to look like it was thrown away garbage, then hid it beneath the locomotive.

We then walked to the truck, and I called the three girls over. Just as I suspected, when they began to walk out of the alley, an adult beggar perked up like a hungry lion, and began to follow the girls as they walked towards us.

As the girls approached I yelled at the man behind them.

"I didn't call you!"

"But?"

As he began to give a phony excuse for following, I cut off his words.

"But nothing, go away, and mind your own business." As he turned and walked away mumbling, the girls shook their heads and laughed.

"Is he a 'bad person'?" I asked.

"Yes!" They all replied, as they all rolled there eyes is disgust.

"I thought so."

While Melissa and I both knelt down to say our good-byes, I could see several of the adult beggars staring at us to see if we gave them money. I then told the girls "Did you know that I asked around town and found out that your birthdays are today."

"What?" they giggled, then sheepishly covered their smiles with their hands to hide their imperfect teeth.

"Yes, all three of you were born on the same day, just different years."

They continued to laugh as I said, "So Melissa and I have a birthday gift for you all, but we don't want anybody to see us give it to you, so I hid it."

When I said "I did not want anybody to see us give it to you", they rolled their eyes again, knowing that if the gift was seen by the others, it would be stolen seconds after we leave.

As I said "I will tell you were I hid the gift," they all moved in closer to hear me whisper. I softly said so the others could not hear. "Do you know where the big locomotive is?"

"Yes," they all replied.

"I put your birthday gift in a paper bag and hid it underneath the locomotive."

"Now listen carefully, this is what I want you to do."

"After we say goodbye, go back to where you were sitting, if anybody asks you what we were talking about, say we were asking for directions. Then after a few minutes, walk over to the locomotive and get the gift. Remember that it is in a brown paper bag, it looks like garbage but it is not. Melissa and I will sit in the car and wait until you return safely with it. But when you return, remember not to wave to us, or talk to us, so the others do not realize we gave you something."

"Got that?" I said with a hint of seriousness for their own safety.

"Yes, we will sit down for a few minutes, then sneak over and find the gift, then come back. Ohh, and don't talk to you when we get back."

"Perfect!"

"But we can quickly say goodbye now." Melissa said. And three warm little hugs later, we parted ways. Melissa and I sat in the truck pretending to read a map as the older beggars approached the girls to figure out why we were all talking so long. I heard her say, "They were looking for directions," and when the older beggars saw us with a map, they believed her.

The girls carried out my orders as if trained soldiers. They sat for a few minutes, before "aimlessly" wandering towards the locomotive, then they disappeared behind it. A few of the adult beggars seemed curious of where they were going, but quickly lost interest when they found a new group of travelers to harass.

About two minutes later I saw three huge smiles coming from around the locomotive. Looking like the cats that ate the canaries, they grinned ear to ear, while uncontrollably giggling like young girls should.

With a look of overwhelming excitement on their faces, their eyes seemed to be uncontrollably drawn to us as they fought to pretend we were not there. It was almost as if they needed to look at us. While they carried out my "orders" almost perfectly, there was one order they did not follow. When they saw that the adult beggars were preoccupied with other people, they all hopped up on the truck's step panel, stuck their heads in our window, and whispered, "Thank you, nice people."

"You are welcome sweethearts, but you better go in case they see you." Melissa and I both said as if it were a pre-planned script. We were trying to smile through tears, while these little ones just had smiles. They know no other way of life.

They all quickly patted Melissa on her hand while saying thank you again, then they continued down the busy sidewalk until they became a part of the bustling crowd.

It is baffling how our planet possesses so many natural riches, and yet we still create a world that determines one's level of happiness, safety, and quality of life to the amount of thin sheets of colored paper (money) they have. Money dictates our lives.

Although these girls live in one of the most beautiful parts of the world, they are forced to believe that there is nothing more valuable than that colored paper. It will be the only way they can survive in their world.

But money does hold a mystical power for its owner. I witnessed this when they came to the truck and whispered "thank you". They seemed like "newer" children. Their smiles were brighter, their posture was straighter, and their eyes sparkled like Mosi-oa-Tunya - the Smoke that Thunders.

Several years have past since that day, and I still wonder what has become of the girls. I am sure it is a question that will never be answered, so I seek comfort in believing that our gift made a part of their lives easier. Whenever I think of Victoria Falls, the girls' smiles shine brightly in my mind.

Since my daughter Ayla was born, I think of them more than ever. On many nights, as I tuck Ayla into her warm bed, I wonder how Kambo, Mudiwa, and Chipo are doing. Are they hungry, are they warm, ...are they alive?

Chapter XII

The Restaurant

I sped over the grooves in the road while my tires tapped an even beat like a metronome. The heat intensified throughout the afternoon and it felt as if I was driving towards the sun. The skin on my arm tightened from hours of direct sun exposure as it hung outside the truck window.

Within the middle of nowhere I encountered people strolling along the edges of the road. They all gave friendly waves and bright smiles as I passed, and then the diamond mine from which they were walking home broke up the dry South African landscape. As I approached the mines, the wind blew a cloud of dust over the road making it difficult to see. The dust was kimberlite, the ore from which diamonds are extracted.

These mines reminded me of a conversation I had with two gentlemen in South Africa's capital city of Johannesburg several days prior. It was at an exclusive four-star Thailand restaurant. Yes, a four-star "Thai" restaurant in Africa, and it is one of the world's finest.

That is what is unique about South Africa, one afternoon you may be eating ostrich from a fire pit outside a house made of cattle dung and mud, then within a few hours drive, dine at a restaurant with a dress code as strict as any eatery on New York City's Madison Avenue.

The two gentlemen sat at the table next to me during dinner. After striking up a conversation with them I learned that one man was the son of a black African diamond mine worker, and the other was a white retired South African soldier.

Throughout dinner our small talk evolved into an enlightening education on how life on the "Dark Continent" can be challenging for both races.

"Few realize how most diamonds are originally obtained" the miner's son said matter of factly. "It is diamond workers like my father that sift through the kimberlite twelve hours a day finding the very mineral that creates a billion dollar industry for the 'civilized' world."

"The sadness is, that most of the world buys this crystallized carbon in the form of jewelry, symbolizing care and compassion towards their loved ones. Most do not comprehend that thousands of miles away, hungry workers toil over 12 hours a day for roughly $20.00 a week in pay. Many mines have been accused of imprisoning workers until they filled their quota for the week and I have heard rumors about enslaving children for free labor."

As I drove past the mine I saw that they were surrounded with razor wire sealing off forbidden zones. I had been warned never to stop my car near a mine or take any photographs of the facilities. Undoubtedly the very road I was driving on is viewed by many of their surveillance cameras.

I once asked a South African government official, "Could an unemployed African begin his own enterprise mining diamonds?" The answer was no. Why? It is believed that it would cause illicit diamond buying. In South Africa there is a law prohibiting 'Illicit Diamond Buying' or IDB. Any rough diamond found on public land must be sold to the government who then resells it to a consolidated mining company, which has the exclusive buying rights for the whole country.

Many Africans I have spoken to are amazed to learn that diamonds are openly traded on the streets of New York City; that activity would guarantee imprisonment in South Africa.

With a visual "tag-team slap of the hands," he turned the conversation over to his friend by smiling and saying to him,

"But, we all have our crosses to bear, don't we?"

The retired officer smiled back and said, "Yes we do, yes we do."

"Do you have a depressing story?" I asked the officer as he wiped his mouth clean with a table napkin.

"My negative experiences living in Africa have been more a matter of bad timing," he said as he squinted one eye and aimed his cigarette over a struck match. After exhaling a thick cloud of gray smoke he said, "I retired from the military and purchased a farm in Kenya. I farmed sisal which is a natural fiber like burlap or hemp. I successfully farmed over 500-acres for three years, until the day a minister in the Office of the President called on black Kenyans to follow the lead taken by landless Zimbabweans, and occupy white-owned farms. That night was the worst night of my life."

"Three o'clock in the morning I awoke to screams and machine gun fire. A mob was yelling my name while spraying machine gun bullets through my front door. They came to kill me and take over my farm. As they beat down my front door, I heard my servant who was from the same tribe as the mob, get shot to death trying to protect me. Many of the men were calling me by name and screaming for me to come out. Several of the men used to work for me so they knew where I slept. Bullets shot through the floor while several men began charging up the steps. They had flashlights taped to the barrels of their guns. To this day, I can close my eyes and see the beam of their lights bouncing off my walls as they cut through the gunpowder smoke."

"I barricaded my bedroom door with a dresser then grabbed the machine gun I kept near my bed. I backed myself into a corner and rolled a huge steel safe in front of me. I grabbed the phone next to me and called the local police. I told them what was happening they said, 'We are sorry but we don't have any cars on duty this shift. But if you come and pick us up we would be glad to assist you.' As I slammed the phone to the floor the mob began beating on my door screaming for me to open it. I rested the gun barrel on the safe and took chest level aim at the door. Just as they broke the door in, I fired on them with over 100 rounds. Every man at the door fell upon the other in a twisted pile, never to terrorize again. The rest of the men on the ground floor heard my retaliating gunfire and fled out into the night like a band of shadowy demons."

"I knew they would return, so I grabbed everything I could fit in my truck, and fled under the cover of darkness to South Africa."

"Later that weekend I learned through the Kenyan newswire, that the mob returned an hour later and burned my house to the ground, thinking I was still in it. Then they set fire to all 500 acres of crops. I never quite understood why they burned everything down. They cut off their nose to spite their face. Now they have control of a farm with no house or crops, I heard it was literally turned into five hundred acres of barren dirt. They will probably turn it into another slum, and they will be in the exact position they were in when they started. Better yet, the mob made such an inferno of my house, that the fire consumed all the dead bodies inside. The jackasses are convinced they killed me, and I sleep well keeping it that way. But I would never accuse them of being intelligent."

I sped past the mines and watched the kimberlite dust swirl in my rear view mirror like a gang of midget tornadoes, I then realized that when it comes to violence and disregard for life, humans are not prejudiced.

Frightful - my peregrine falcon

A red-tailed hawk (juvenile)

My European eagleowl - three-weeks old

My European eagleowl - six-weeks old

My European eagleowl as an adult.

A screech owl that once lived in my bedroom.

My Andean condor at six-months old.

My Andean condor at three-years old.

An Acacia tree - *Zimbabwe, Africa*

A typical African road - *Zimbabwe, Africa*

Baboons leaving a watering hole - *Zimbabwe, Africa*

A Burchell's Zebra - *Zimbabwe, Africa*

A Burchell's Zebra grazing - *Zimbabwe, Africa*

Zimbabwe boys driving a cart which is pulled by
donkeys.. Notice the word *Toyota* is painted
on the back.

A baboon skull (on top) and a wildebeest skull (on bottom) - *Zimb*
This is exactly how I found them.
A native must have placed the baboon skull on top of the wildebeest

An African lion - *South Africa*

A giraffe - *Zimbabwe, Africa*

Several of my friends from *Botswana, Africa*

An ostrich - *Kalahari desert, South Africa*

Gemsbok - *Kalahari desert, South Africa*

A Jackal - *Kalahari desert, South Africa*

African Elephants - Zimbabwe, *Africa*

A one-tusked African elephant rubbing its body on a rock.
The tusk must have broken off during a fight.

An African elephant inspecting me with his trunk.

A lone bull elephant - Zimbabwe, Africa

Elephant X-ing - Zimbabwe, Africa

Mosi-oa-Tunya - *Victoria Falls, Zimbabwe*
The white spot in the upper right corner is a person.

Diamond mine workers - *South Africa*

Myself approaching *Montserrat* by boat.

A jagged cliff on the north end of *Montserrat*.

A mural honoring the Montserrat oriole. - *Salem, Montserrat*

A party in an old abandoned sugar cane mill. - *Montserrat*

A volcanic eruption - photographed from the back porch of my guesthouse - *Montserrat*

Falling volcanic ash turning day into night.
Montserrat

A dying forest within the shadow of the volcano. - *Montserrat*

"Ground Zero", Soufriere Hills volcano - *Montserrat*
Notice the pyroclastic flow pouring out of it's side.

The ravished capital of *Plymouth, Montserrat*

Roofs cave in as the volcanic ash hardens like concrete.

f the homes still have their owners belonging in them, just as if they had left their house to go shopping for the afternoon.
Pirates often come ashore and pillage what was left behind.

One of the many abandoned million dollar homes.
Plymouth, Montserrat

Hotels and condos near the volcano were also abandoned.
Montserrat

A utility truck engulfed by a volcanic mudflow. - *Montserrat*

What is now left of *Montserrat's* golf course.

Rendezvous Beach - *Montserrat*

A gharial

feared 20-foot long crocodilian is rather harmless, having a diet consisting mostly of fish.

A puff adder

Melissa watching T.V. with a 15-foot python.

A sea lion

A very inquisitive tiger friend.

Chapter XIII

The Emerald Dragon
Montserrat - West Indies

"What is your final destination?" I was asked upon entering Antiguan customs.

"Montserrat," I replied.

While searching my bags the customs agent commented, "Do you know you're running the wrong way?"

He then added with a smirk, "Why do you want to go there? "

As I handed him my passport, I responded, "To watch the volcano erupt." While stamping my documents, he shook his head and directed me to the boat.

The small volcanic island of Montserrat forms part of

the Leeward Island chain in the West Indies, a geologically young archipelago that began forming less than 50 million years ago. The island's volcano has remained dormant for some four-hundred years but all that changed in July of 1995. The Emerald Dragon awoke in a very cranky mood.

The eruptions involved intense earthquake swarms. Steam exploded out of the mountain from the rapid heating of ground water by the rising magma. By mid-November of that year, the magma reached the surface and a new lava dome began to form. The lava of Caribbean volcanoes is known as andesite and is very viscous, thick like honey. It piles up around the volcano's vent, forming a dome that continues to rebuild and collapse. When the dome collapses it creates a pyroclastic flow which is an avalanche of millions of tons of fragmented lava and incandescent gasses that race down the mountainside destroying everything in its path. Reaching speeds over 100-mph and temperatures over 600 degrees Celsius, nothing within its reach survives.

As a result of the island's violent outbursts, two thirds of this forty square mile landmass became unlivable. Called the Exclusion Zone, entering it without direct government permission and escort is illegal.

A large-scale evacuation effort relocated over 8,000 of the 11,000 residents. Most people searched for a better life on a neighboring island or in England which is Montserrat's "mother country."

After learning that the Montserrat volcano was con

sidered one of the world's most dangerous volcanoes, I flew down to the island to see how its wildlife and ecosystem reacted to this destructive environment.

As a result of the volcanic activity, Montserrat's airport was demolished, so I rode the island's ferry from Antigua. After climbing aboard the 150-foot boat I realized that there were only nine other people on deck. All of them were Montserrat natives returning after a day of shopping in Antigua. These are some of the resilient few who have toughed out the volcano's wrath and refuse to leave their homes.

The boat was a high powered catamaran, unlike any ferry I have seen. It transports people to and from the island twice a day and is on stand by in case of an evacuation, that is if the sea permits it to do so; some days when the sea swells are too treacherous the boat cannot safely dock in Montserrat's Little Bay. In order to keep the boat finely tuned, the Captain ran it at full speed.

As we departed Antigua, I realize that if this were the United States we would have had at least 15-minutes of "safety instruction." Here I appreciated the "use your head" approach; if you did not use your head, you would find yourself swimming. The sea was so rough, even some of the seasoned passengers held on for dear life.

The splashing water and chop of the boat digging into the waves was unusually peaceful. Fatigued from traveling over 2,000 miles before noon, I felt as if I was in a dream state. The bright sun made everything overly sharp and vivid. The crystal blue water rolled by and the sweet smell of the Caribbean air relaxed me like a dentist's laughing gas.

In this part of the world fish can fly. In small squadrons, they soared over the waves like diamonds being skipped over the sea. Then their wings would cut into a wave, plunging them into the abyss like mini kamikaze pilots. I pictured little "rising sun" headbands around each of their tiny heads.

Far in the distance the faint silhouette of Montserrat emerged from the horizon. The reflection of the water made the island appear to hover in mid air as its volcano hung from the sky shrouded in clouds. When the boat approached the north end of the island considered the "Safe-Zone," lush aloe trees and palms gave a glimpse of what the entire island was like before the eruptions.

Like the islands from Jurassic Park and King Kong, Montserrat puts forth a menacing aura as its craggy cliffs jut out of the Caribbean Sea. Its thick jungle vegetation hides a force uncomprehendable to most humans, a far greater power than Hollywood could ever dream up.

When the boat pulled up to the dock, a dozen or so people lined the shore waiting to depart the island on the boat's return trip to Antigua. While being cleared through customs, I could not help but notice that everybody seemed unconcerned and happy. The tiny bar next to the custom's pavilion was perfectly named The Last Resort. It was full of customers drinking their beer, along with lightly tapping one another's fists together in a sign of respect.

The Last Resort is owned and operated by a man named Moose. Moose's staff consists of his lovely wife plus his two extremely well behaved and hard working children. The spear fishermen are still wet when they deliver the catch of the day. On most evenings I would watch the sunset from Moose's and enjoy a wonderful home cooked meal. While eating, a gang of the largest, thickest, and most intimidating black and yellow spiders paced like intoxicated tight rope walkers over my head. They always seemed as if they were about to fall on me but they never did. I actually became rather used to them being there and eventually developed the habit of holding them. They were rather docile, with their long legs straddling my entire hand but never biting. Moose welcomes the spiders just as much as his customers.

After passing through customs, I met my contact from Montserrat's Emergency Department and he drove me to my guesthouse. The island's roads are cut out of the sides of the mountains and all the cars chirp their tires as they wind their way up the steep thin hills.

My rented guesthouse sat next to the governor's home, overlooking the Caribbean Sea, on the edge of the "Exclusion Zone". On my return trips to the island I continued to stay in this same house. Aside from it being a luxurious house, it is logistically perfect. This beautiful location is completely surrounded by jungle except for the view of the crystal blue Caribbean Sea. It is so close to the Exclusion zone that watching the eruptions from the back deck gave me a stiff neck. It is like watching an IMAX movie while sitting in the front row.

Once I settled all of my gear in the house, I decided to venture into the small town of Salem. This town lies in the shadow of the volcano and was considered part of the Exclusion Zone for some time but had recently reopened. It was a 3-mile walk into the town and it was pitch dark, not a street light and, on that night, not even the moon.

I have quickly learned from experience that in many areas of the world it is not wise to venture out after dark. Montserrat is the exception; it has little or no crime. When the island began its evacuation there were only eight prisoners in their jail. The police commissioner once told me of a small group of bank robbers that he incarcerated. When most people think of bank robberies, we envision people in Nixon masks wildly pointing guns and cursing. Not on Montserrat.

This is how they robbed a bank. When a pyroclastic flow covered their capital city of Plymouth, several of their banks were also covered. A small group of men learned that during the hectic evacuation of the city, one of the banks left behind one million dollars in uncirculated cash. So one night they hiked down to Plymouth, dug a tunnel through the hard ash, broke into the bank, and stole the loot. I imagine that they might have gotten away with the deed except for the fact that they tried to exchange all the money at once in a casino in Antigua. Being uncirulated bills, the robbers were quickly caught. So even most crimes in Montserrat are peaceful.

Whether poor or a millionaire, everyone leaves their homes open, their car doors unlocked, and no one bothers a thing. This was also a rule before their ongoing tragedy. I have found that most of the residents on Montserrat are very proud people and have very little class envy.

As I was walking into Salem, all I heard were the digital sounds of tree frogs at a deafening volume. About a half mile from the town, I saw the single headlight of a motorcycle coming toward me at a high rate of speed. I was a bit more nervous than I normally would have been, due to the fact that there are no drinking and driving laws in Montserrat, and no speed limits.

A dark, massive creature emerged from the weeds about 50 feet in front of me, it charged the motorcycle and "BLAM!" The bike then crashed onto the road. As the bike hit the pavement the gas tank flew to the left, the seat flew off to the right, and the driver's body was sent skidding down the middle of the road. Just as quickly as the dark creature appeared, it vanished.

I ran to help the man as residents emerged from their homes to see what was going on. Being totally baffled by the event I asked, "What happened?". One Rastafarian man next to me said, "Ya mon, de bulls, they no like de sound of de bike, so da charge".

The bulls roamed free after the eruptions began since most of the farmers had relocated off the island. The bulls hate the loud noise of the motorcycles and will occasionally go head to head with them The bull always walks away and the rider flies away. After we dusted off the injured biker, he got a lift to a local doctor to be examined. Later, I found out he survived suffering only a broken collarbone and fractured wrist.

I began speaking to some of the residents at the accident scene and they invited me to a local pub called Jimmo's to play a few games of dominoes. Dominoes is a very intense game for them, almost a contact sport. The more confident they are of their move, the harder they slam the domino on the table. When I would play against them, I could always guess who the big winner of the day was because the rickety table leaned in his direction from being slapped so much.

During the games, the men traded stories back and forth about growing up on the island, what it was like in the past, and their hopes for the future. They spoke of when their ancestors were alive and the volcano was as active as it is today. One could see the fiery glow of the magma emitted from the cone of the volcano. They would tell the children that is where Jack O'Lantern lives and if you are bad, he will run down and take you away. Much like many societies, the children behave due to the fear of a higher power or "boogieman."

Perhaps there could be more to the story. Years ago, around Halloween, four parts of the volcano's dome collapsed, creating what looked like two eyes, a nose and a

mouth which glowed over the island like a carved pumpkin.

I spoke to a man who, before the heavy eruptions,
decided to climb into the volcano. He said that when he
reached the cone it was like entering a separate reality.
Red, blue and orange fireballs would hover in the air, then
shoot across the cavern only to hover again and dart back
like angry ghosts. It was the incandescent gasses burning
away within the cone.

At 6:30 a.m. the following morning, I was awakened
by what I thought was thunder. Still half asleep, I assumed
that a fierce thunderstorm was passing by. Then Richard,
the owner of the house yelled, "Wake up! We've got an
eruption!"

As continuous loud explosions rang out, I took a second and scrambled for my camera. After I ran out to the
back porch, I stared at a 20,000 foot high ash cloud hanging over my head. As the hot ash and gas shot towards the
sky, it slowly blocked out the sun. For the next half-hour I
photographed the plume and watched the wind blow the
ash west where it splashed down into the sea in front of
the house. Good Morning!

When the volcano settled, I traveled with the chief of
the Emergency Department to see what path the pyroclastic flow had taken. We discovered that the flow burned its
way down the Tar River straight out to sea, barely missing
the already ravaged airport. The Tar River area is one of
the two most common paths for the pyroclastic flows.

We wandered near the airport and saw smoke rising from the barren ground where the flow had traveled. The airport is built on an ancient Caribbean Indian burial ground. Many natives feel that the eruptions are the gods punishment for disturbing such sacred grounds.

That afternoon the government of Montserrat invited me into the Exclusion Zone. It was a last minute decision by the police commissioner because of the heavy volcanic activity that morning. Since the island's radio station issues volcano warnings regularly, he required us to listen to the radio while in the dangerous areas.

I remember the emotions I had going into the Exclusion Zone. Entering a place that has defeated man, and is continuing to do so, was a feeling few people ever get to experience. No matter how much power, money or connections one has, he is still a proverbial ant to the volcano and can be eliminated in seconds. It is human nature to thrive on the sense of control, but here, control is not an option.

The Chief of Defense opened the gate and we drove into an environment beyond imagination. The only visible life were a few nervous lost dogs whose owners were forced to abandoned them during the evacuation. Otherwise, it was deathly quiet, a ghost town. Even our car silently coasted over the morning's freshly fallen ash like snow.

The dead forests resembled giant toothpicks thrown in the ash. A suffocating sensation overcame me as I saw the slumping ash encased vegetation, wilting and choking, unable to produce oxygen. Resembling the outer edges of a nuclear blast, everything was intact, yet there was nothing. The roofs of once beautiful million dollar homes were caving in from the weight of the rain soaked ash. Their T.V. satellite dishes were reduced to merely giant bowls of ash. The playgrounds were empty. Only the ocean breeze squeaked the childrens swings back and forth. The soul of this town had left along with its people.

When we stopped on the side of the road, I realized that my official driver had switched the car's radio station to a cricket game instead of monitoring the local volcanic warnings. If we received an eruption warning, we would have never known about it. But where we were heading next, we would have no problem knowing if another eruption was set in motion.

For a short distance we walked through a dry dead forest until we arrived at a cliffside, and there stood Soufriere Hills volcano. I smelled the volcano as it leaked clouds of sulfuric gas from its vents. In its presence, I felt like we should whisper or say nothing. Words had no place here.

Boulders the size of school buses lay where they had poured out from its side. Nineteen farmers died here when she first began to erupt. I could barely see the tiers where the farmers grew their crops up her side. I had no problem picturing these gentle people tending to their fields moments before the volcano consumed them.

Off to the left lay the remains of entire villages covered with five to fifteen feet of ash that had hardened like concrete after it rained. A local journalist stood next to me trying to find where her house once stood. She failed to find it. All of the landmarks she once used to locate her property in the past were all now gone, either buried or burnt away.

From there we drove on to Plymouth, the former capital. From a distance Plymouth looks like the ancient ruins of a society that had deserted the area hundreds of years ago, except here, future archeologists will excavate microwaves and cars instead of pottery and hand tools.

Plymouth was the hub of activity for the entire island until 1995 when a pyroclastic flow descended from the volcano, forever destroying it in a matter of seconds. Their church is now just a shell of stone. Amidst all the rubble stands the altar with a brass chalice melted to the top of it.

Most three-story buildings looked like single floor structures since the two lower stories were engulfed in ash and rock. I thought back to the people who had lived there and wondered if they had any clue that the mountain directly over them would soon awake, altering or destroying their lives in seconds.

Within the ash were small rivers leading to the sea, etched by rain running off the volcano. With each new storm, the landscape changes. In one area of Plymouth, a new "river" ran through a cemetery, washing the dead into the sea.

In some areas small patches of grass struggled to exist despite the harsh environment. Only grasses with shallow roots have any chance of survival. Long after a pyroclastic flow, one can probe a few meters into the ash and find it can still be up to 600 degrees.

After silently standing over this lost city, we felt we had pushed our luck far enough and decided to head back into the Safe Zone. With one more eyeful of the volcano etched in my mind, we left.

Even with all the destruction the volcano caused, I did not feel ill towards it - just respect. There I was in a place that was unsuitable, unstable and uncaring for all life, yet I did not want to leave. Standing next to something of such brutal force and energy gave me an adrenaline rush that could not be matched. I now see why many cultures worship volcanoes, deeming them gods or god-like. They have the power over life or death, demanding respect and breeding fear.

We ventured back through the Safe Zone, firmly locking the gate behind us. While leaving the Safe Zone, we arrived at a bridge that had been washed out by a mudslide. Originally, that bridge spanned across a ravine over 40 feet deep. When heavy rains mixed with the volcanic ash, it created a mudslide that filled the entire riverbed. It went over the bridge and demolished the adjacent golf course covering it with ash and boulders, leaving it to resemble the surface of the moon. A utility truck lay submerged up to its windows in dried mud and rocks.

The next morning I hiked up a small mountain near the volcano to search for the endangered Montserrat Oriole. This bird lives exclusively on Montserrat and its population has been decimated from habitat loss due to agriculture, hurricane Hugo, and strike three is the volcanic activity. Some estimates state that over 76% of their habitat has been destroyed. Most of the losses are concentrated in the ghauts, (French for gullies), prime habitat for the oriole and essential for their survival.

It is a realistic scenario that with the continuation of the eruptions, it is not likely that a viable population will survive over 50 years. There is a 50:50 chance of total extinction within 10 to 15 years.

The day was dark and drizzly. A thick layer of cottony clouds covered the mountaintops and hung in front of the volcano like a theater curtain. Thick jungle foliage held the rain of the night's passing storm, and it showered down on me as I weaved through the rainforest.

Beyond a tiny knoll of green ferns and moss, I heard rushing water and birds chirping. I slowly sneaked over the knoll and peered between two ferns that I separated with my hands. A crystal clear mountain stream poured over the jagged rocks into a small pool surrounded by a thick carpet of moss. The coal black hue of the rich soil contrasted a dark outline around the moss while the shallow roots of various plants gripped the earth like long fingers. Pinkish flowers hung over the pool, and their leaves reached out like arms, catching the mist of the tiny water fall. A black and yellow *Heliconius* butterfly fluttered among the flowers. It landed on each of the flowers, weighing them down enough to cause the blossoms to jiggle like empty bells. Minuscule bugs gently skimmed the surface of the water. It was hard to distinguish whether they were flying, and occasionally touched the water, or were swimming and occasionally lifted from the water. Tiny "unknowns" scrambled within the ferns causing the leaves to shake as if the whole plant was silently chuckling. I continued to lie on my stomach hidden in the ferns, hoping to catch a glimpse of a Montserrat Oriole drinking or bathing. I watched and listened.

The next time you are around a rushing stream, listen to it. You will be able to hear the sound of every musical note being played together. And unlike any instrument, playing every note at once is always soothing to those around it.

Within a few minutes several birds that looked as if they were dressed for a Mardi Gras parade, slipped down from the trees to bath. As they preened their feathers at the outer edge of the pool, a buzzing sound filled the air. Then out from the forest's morning fog, a hummingbird sped over to one of the flowers, and quickly inserted its beak into it with a surgeon's precision.

Its local name is the Doctor Bird, but it is generally called a Purple-throated Carib. This brilliant looking bird is largely black with purplish red patches, a bluish green tail, and metallic green wings.

To keep his "clothes" glowing he must conserve energy. With a brain the size of a grain of rice, this 5-inch long "Liberace" must remember to never return to the same blossom twice. Wasting vital energy on empty flowers could mean certain death for a hummingbird.

When done drinking from all the flowers, he faced me and hovered in mid air. Like a disco ball he rotated, reflecting tiny beads of waterfall mist that gathered on him. After the short hover break he turned his back to me and streaked though the rainforest like a psychedelic tracer bullet.

As soon as the hummingbird flew out of sight, BOOM!!! The volcano erupted! Explosions rang out one after another as if an air raid of bombs were being dropped upon a single target.

I jumped out from under the ferns and sprinted down the mountain. Fighting to stay on the thin path, I began tripping over the pointy rocks and slipping on the moss. Within five minutes (probably a new world record) I was out of the forest and in a tiny field next to a small dirt road.

I looked to the sky and saw a 20,000-foot tall ash cloud. Identical to the mushroom cloud of a nuclear bomb, it grew towards the sky as its glowing molten "root" churned and roared within the earth. As if a temper tantrum from a mythical god, lightening shot out from the cone and thunder vibrated the ground.

At a temperature over 6,000 degrees, the explosion was

so immense that it immediately created its own weather system. Before the eruption, it was drizzling. During the initial eruption, the volcano produced thunder and lightening. Minutes later it became clear, sunny perfect beach weather. The sun shone and the only visible cloud in the sky was rooted to the earth and stood over 30,000 feet tall. Although it seemed like perfect weather, the wildlife knew otherwise. Not a bird chirped, nor a frog croaked.

I began to jog up to Salem as the ash plume thickened and began to block out the sun. As it billowed above my head, the temperature dropped about ten degrees and the town darkened. Then it began to rain, not water, but rocks and ash.

At first the fine ash falls. It is so fine one does not even realize its falling, except it makes your eyes itch as if you have hayfever. Then the gravely ash falls like black snow that never melts. I placed my respirator over my face and continued to jog. One learns to take this little filtered mask with you everywhere in Montserrat. Breathing the ash from this volcano can cause *Silicosis*, also known as Black lung.

The gravely ash started mixing with rain, but it was not an ordinary rain it was sulfuric acid. The volcano vents sulfuric gasses into the atmosphere. Then, while in the atmosphere, hydrogen sulfide and sulfur dioxide mix and undergo a set of chemical reactions, eventually combining with water to produce sulfuric acid, major acid rain.

Montserrat's acid rain is so concentrated and intense,

that it is a prime location to study the effects of acid rain. Acid rain greatly affects Montserrat's diverse terrestrial habitats, such as the coastal mangroves, semi-desert vegetation, and the cloud forest. Acid rain affects plants by breaking down the lipids and protective membranes of their foliage, which leads to their death.

Soon the ash totally blocked out the sun's rays and the town went black as night. The only sounds were honking of car horns and the "spine-chilling" squeal of car windshield wipers scratching the fallen ash over their windows.

I made it to a small store in Salem where I waited out the falling ash and talked with some of the natives. One gentleman said "Ahh, tis I're mon, tis nuttin.": translation "Ahh, It is alright man, this is nothing." It has become such a common occurrence for them, that they seem rather more annoyed with the volcano, than scared of it. When the falling ash began to thin, I tightened my respirator to my face and jogged back to my house.

Later that evening I discovered the volcano's acid rain had rotted the metal clips off my boots. Then after my wristwatch corroded off my arm, I noticed the acid rain also fused the watch's dive gauge.

The volcano is a very domineering force, and overshadows Montserrat's inner beauty, but adds to the island's mystique. It is a microcosm of how people can work together in a time of immense destruction and desperation, and yet still remain happy, helpful, respectful, and caring.

On the bright side the volcano has kept the island free

of annoying, disrespectful tourists. There is only one white sand beach on the whole island, and one can only arrive there by a mile hike over a mountain or by boat. I made it my own paradise, spending entire days diving among its coral reef watching thousands of schooling fish and the occasional passing shark, then napping on the white sand without ever seeing another human soul.

It became my hideaway, and I return there as much as life allows me. If you ever get the urge to see the way life should be lived, visit the "Emerald Dragon", then ask around for me if I am not at the beach, check Moose's.

The Twilight of the Wild

Chapter XIV

Fear of theUnknown

"Every alligator over five feet long should be shot!" This statement has been repeated by a number of Florida residents and government officials. They feel this action would lessen the threat of people being attacked by alligators within the state.

A concerned Florida resident contacted me with this information and my response was, "How common are alligator attacks in Florida?" My research concluded that an average of 15 to 20 non-fatal attacks take place per year.

Only 15 to 20 people; what is the big deal? That is roughly a one in a million chance of attack. Everyday Americans certainly take greater risks with far worse odds.

So why do so many people become hysterical when faced with such a threat? It is the instinctual human response called fear of the unknown. Fear of the unknown is a commanding force that we all possess. It has reached out and clutched its bony fingers around the throats of many people, cultures, and species, ultimately choking the life from them all. It magnifies our mind's sense of paranoia, then shrinks our confidence and blinds all rational thought. Whether in a Los Angles ghetto or a Florida swamp, fear of the unknown controls each of its victims with an equally iron fist.

It convinces our mind that the unreasonable is reasonable. For example, between 1948 and 1999 there have been approximately 248 confirmed alligator attacks on humans in the State of Florida. Only nine incidents were fatal, that is nine too many as far as the victims' families are concerned. But in 1998 alone, 967 murders, 7,404 rapes, 95,447 assaults, and 887,107 robberies took place within the Sunshine State. Humans carried out every single one of those crimes and yet we naturally distrust the alligator more then our fellow humans.

Sharks fall within the same undesirable social class as alligators. Unfortunately, this became more prominent after the 1975 movie release of *JAWS*. Although one of my favorite movies, its plot did create hysteria with the uninformed public, leaving many beaches barren of swimmers and the shark branded an evil killer. The truth is that for every five humans killed by sharks, 100 million sharks are killed by humans.

"Man's best friend" bites 500,000 to 1 million Americans annually, severely enough to require medical attention. In addition, countless more dog bites go unreported and untreated.

Machines kill more humans than any animal has. In 1999, 37,000 Americans were killed by motor vehicles. Yet the very next year Americans purchased over 15 million more of these "death traps", and most people remain worry-free as they are propelled faster and faster to their destinations.

Approximately every 115-minutes a train collides with a person or vehicle within the United States. Yet their tracks continue to weave their way throughout the "fruited plain".

But to top it all, in 1996, 43,687 Americans were injured by their toilets! I do not know how, I do not want to know how, although malfunctions in water pressure have caused certain types of toilets to explode, hurling ceramic shrapnel at anyone in the bathroom. Yet I have witnessed no toilet shooting sprees, nor society running back to the old reliable out-house.

Humans fear machines less than animals because we have co-existed with machines for only several hundred years. It is not nearly enough time to instill a fear of them within our subconscious.

For over three million years humans have been in direct contact with animals. At one point in time or another, we have either competed with them for food and living space or we have been considered by them as objects of prey.

Even the most compassionate individual carries the fear of the unknown in their ancestral baggage. But give one the opportunity to be exposed to wild animals, the gates of understanding will swing open and the creature's vital place within nature can be seen and appreciated.

But if time persists as it has and the technological age forces society's workplace to continue replacing human souls with "silicon souls" direct competition with machines is imminent.

Humans are the most unpredictable creatures on earth. Yet we tolerate our faults because they exist within our own kind. But let an outsider, like an alligator, attempt the same deed and it better beware. The situation is very political in a way.

Nothing proved to be more true than when I was asked to give a speech at The American Museum of Natural History in New York City. In order to bring my animals to the museum, I had to obtain a permit from a division of the New York City Board of Health, cleverly nicknamed the "Rat-bite Department". While I was in the process of filing for the permit, I became intrigued with New York City's rat situation.

I learned that the population of rats in New York City is greater than the population of people, the rats just hide better. I also learned that there are roughly 150 reports a year filed involving rat bites. The number of reports filed where humans bit other humans, is over 1,000 per year. It is estimated that every year New Yorkers bite ten times more people than the rats do, yet we are still more afraid of the rats.

But fear of the unknown has its purpose. It makes us cautious in unpredictable situations and strives to keep us intact. The key is not to employ it as a weapon, but as a shield.

The Twilight of the Wild

Chapter XV

The Serpent

"Try this one", the african native said as he brushed sand away from the entrance of an animal's burrow. His partner dropped a canvas bag from his shoulder and pulled a long piece of cloth from it. He then sat on the ground while wrapping his foot and leg in a cocoon of cloth. When the leg was entirely wrapped, he slid it into the hole.

Within minutes his leg flinched and he yelled, "He took!". After ten minutes the old man became restless and began to drip with sweat. "Now, now!" he yelled. His partner grabbed him by the arms and tried to drag him out of the hole. The old man seemed overly heavy as his buddy struggled to obtain his footing on the loose ground. After getting a good foothold, he pulled the old man out of the hole to expose a giant python trying to eat his leg. The snake had swallowed his entire leg up to the middle of his thigh.

The snake was over eighteen-foot long and weighed 150 lbs. As it thrashed around, the old man spread his arms out on the sand to keep his balance. His partner wrestled the snake's body into the canvas bag, then began to pry the pythons jaws open with his hands. With the snake's jaws held wide open the old man pointed his toes and slowly worked his leg out of the snake's mouth.

That was the seventh snake the old man captured that summer and he never got a scratch. As long as he wraps enough cloth around his leg, the snake's teeth never cut him.

People get woozy and cringe when I tell that story. "Oh my god, I'd rather die," most say. But snakes do not have to engulf a body part to invoke terror within us. Their mere presence is enough to send the most macho of men atop a chair holding his "skirt." Snakes have permeated the subconscious. They unwillingly breed fear and hatred as the overactive human imagination transforms them into a far more evil supernatural being, the mythical serpent.

While lecturing at thousands of schools, I have closely studied human reactions towards snakes. As I reach the segment of my lecture where I discuss snakes, I say, "Raise your hands if you like snakes." Their reactions are very predictable. Most of the children raise their hands with great excitement, and all but a few teachers sit with their hands by their sides while bearing the facial expression of wearing a dirty diaper.

These two different reactions made me conclude that humans must be introduced to snakes as a young child in order to comfortably accept them. Otherwise, there will almost always be some sort of apprehension in the adult.

Most people gravitate toward specific animals because they are cute, cuddly, or resemble us. A snake is none of the above. There is nothing human-like about a snake. They lack arms and legs, yet they mysteriously propel their bodies with great speed and stealth. We rely so much on our legs and arms to exist that it is hard for us to relate to a seemingly "lower" creature that gets along perfectly without them. Snakes do not have moveable eyelids, so they always seem to be staring at you. Many animals, besides humans, have a natural aversion to being stared at; it is considered a threat. Their unique physical features mixed with centuries of myth and religious belief have given snakes the hard task in winning an adult's compassion.

Children have the better reaction because they are in a discovery stage of life and greet the unfamiliar. So if given the opportunity to interact with snakes, children respond much better than adults. The only time the majority of children did not raise their hands in favor of snakes occurs when I lecture within our nation's large cities. Many of these children come from generations of city dwellers and are so far removed from the natural world that they view a wild animal as an alien. Most of their ancestors had never been exposed to snakes which caused this irrational fear to be passed down through the generations.

I was introduced to snakes at the age of six, but with much resistance from my mother. My quest for a snake began in an odd way. I was playing in my backyard when I saw something run underneath my neighbor's car. I slowly crept over to the car and peeked beneath; it was a mouse. I crawled underneath the car and found a mouse staring at me and shaking in fear; it had a broken leg.

"Well, we must fix your leg," I said to the mouse as I reached out to grab it. I managed to corner her against a tire and grab her around the waist. As I heard a high-pitched squeak, she sank her teeth into my thumb. Still determined to help her as she chewed on me, I ran into the house looking for a bucket. After several shakes of my hand, she let go and dropped into the bucket. Proud of my capture I yelled, "Mom!, look what I caught, it bit me; can I keep it?"

I then quickly learned that there are two things you can not say to your mother in the same sentence, "it bit me" and "can I keep it?" While she frantically cleaned my wound she said, "Absolutely not!".

"Well if I can't have a mouse then I want a snake!" I yelled.

My mother did not want me to have a snake. But she also did not want to hear me pester her about not having one. She replied "If you find a snake, remember where it is, go get your dad to check it out, and if it's not poisonous you can keep it." I thought it was a great idea when I was six years old, but years later I realized what she was up to. First of all, it was almost wintertime and she knew I would never find a snake during a cold New York winter. Second, if for some weird reason I did find a snake, it would probably be gone by the time I got my dad. But it backfired on her, she forgot about two things; a six-year-old never forgets, and pet shops.

About two months later my parents took me to a pet shop to buy a goldfish for my sister. When I walked into the store I saw an aquarium against the back wall with snakes. Being the good boy I always was, I did what I was told. I remember where they were, and yelled, "Mom, there's some snakes, there's dad, and they're not poisonous."

With my mom's head spinning, we left with a snake and lots of goldfish to feed the snake. It was a garter snake. I really wanted a king cobra, but I settled.

After many years, "Sam the snake" could have been found sleeping in my shirt, going to school, or roaming my bedroom. Unfortunately, our time together was cut short after he made one too many unauthorized expeditions though our house and my mother took him for a walk in the woods. Only one of them returned.

Sam was my first recollection of interacting with something that was so different than I was, yet just as perfect I thought. My first experiences with Sam made me more open towards the different and unusual, and always having a few snakes around the house helps remind me to continue to do so.

Snakes are truly harmless animals if left alone and given their space. When not, most are still rather tolerant of humans. Whenever I have ended up meeting the "sharp end" of a snake, I deserved it.

I have witnessed two behaviors while approaching wild snakes. They either lie still and try to blend with their surroundings or they speed away. Whenever they slithered right towards me, it was not an attack. The logical explanation is that while searching for prey an inch or two off the ground, the snake most likely did not even realize I was there.

A snake senses are just as unique as their body shape. They have no ears, yet they are not deaf. They detect vibrations from the ground through their lower jawbone which then transfers the vibrations to the small ear bone. These vibrations can tell a snake if another animal is large or small, and if it is coming toward them or going away from them. Snakes feel sound instead of hearing it. So a snake charmer's cobra never hears the flute playing, it just follows the motion as the charmer moves it.

A snake's sense of smell is also different than ours. Snakes taste the air rather than smell it. When a snake investigates its surroundings, it flicks its forked tongue into the air picking up minute chemical particals. The snake then quickly draws its tongue back into its mouth and presses the tip into two openings in the roof of the mouth called the Jacobson's organ. Here tastes and smells are analyzed informing the snake about any nearby predators, prey, or mate.

Since snakes hide easily and detect their surroundings much differently than we do, accidents and unfortunate situations do occur. According to Professor Janis Rose, author of *Coral Snakes of the Americas*, the first casualty of the American Civil War was not as a result of war, but by the bite of an eastern coral snake.

A snake in a bush camp I stayed at in Zimbabwe killed a man. It was a rainy night and two men were sharing a tent. One of the men got out of the tent and forgot to zip the tent's door closed behind him. While outside a puff adder slid into the tent to dry off from the rain. After the man returned to the tent and fell back to sleep, the puff adder slithered over his hand and woke him up. Startled, the man jerked his hand which flung the snake across the tent.

The notoriously fast Puff Adder managed to bite the man twice in the back of the hand as it was flung. To add insult to injury, the peacefully sleeping man the snake landed on received a bite to his leg.

The man bitten in the hand died from the a direct injection into a vein and the man bitten in the leg received a smaller dose of venom since most of it had been injected into his friend. He lived after being picked up by a rescue chopper and spent a few weeks in a hospital.

Knock on wood, I have only had a couple close calls with poisonous snakes.. The most memorable one was a cobra that struck at my leg and got its fangs caught in my pant's leg. As it attempted to inject its venom, I felt it pour down the side of my leg and quickly soaked my pants. It happened because I was not paying proper attention to what I was doing. I now understand why my school report cards always displayed the comment "easily distracted".

But the "Award for Good Luck" should go to a colleague of mine. While he was giving a lecture about rattlesnakes, he was holding a rattler. The snake became startled by an unruly child in the audience and struck at my friend, biting him in the chest. Surprised he did not feel any pain, he looked down at his chest and realized the snake unloaded a lethal dose of venom into a pack of cigarettes he had in his shirt pocket. The venom drenched cigarette pack saved him from a direct bite to the heart which would have guaranteed instant death. He is the only person I know that can say cigarettes saved his life. I think now he will never quit smoking.

But in general, unprovoked attacks are extremely rare, and snakes account for very few human fatalities, only 10 to 15 people a year in the U.S. The vast majority of cases of snakes biting humans involve the abuse of alcohol. Hmm, wonder which of the two is doing the drinking?

Chapter XVI

The Element of Life

Did you know that hiding a bag of dead lobsters, jelly-fish and horseshoe crabs within a car's trunk for over two weeks while on summer vacation, creates an odor that has been known to curl your toenails? I did not know this. Well, at least not on this particular occasion.

I was 7 years old and on my first visit to the New Jersey seashore. Prior to my "first date" with the ocean, I had already acquired a great respect for the water. My grandfather owned a house along the Hudson River where I had spent countless days fishing and exploring. But at that time I never truly knew how powerful, huge and intimidating the ocean was.

While my parents stood behind me, I waded into the Atlantic. It was much colder than I had expected. I walked out into the surf until the water was up past my knees, then dug my toes into the packed sand and challenged my first wave.

As my mother warned "Be careful," I watched a dark blue wave roll towards me. As if a rookie matador, I nervously stood my ground as my "bull" charged. I stood only four foot tall and weighed only sixty-five pounds. This "wall of water" looked like a tsunami to me.

I started to lose my cool and chicken out when the wave rapidly grew before my eyes. As the very tip of the wave began to reach out towards me like a hand, the undertow pulled on my ankles, sucking the beach from beneath my feet.

My parents forewarned me about the undertow, but I never conceived it was so powerful. The very same force that pulled on my toothpick legs was the same force that is able to grab an entire house and feed it to the sea as quickly as a mother spoon-feeds her baby. The sea is able to split apart the largest ocean liners just as effortlessly as it floats a starfish onto the beach.

Just as I became terrified that the undertow was going to suck me into the Abyss, my over-matched opponent "freight-lined" me smack in the face. It was a liquid punch.

Like a double-teamed tackle, the undertow knocked my feet out from under me while the wave hit from the front. I was thrown to the sand as the wave steamrolled over me.

Being assaulted by water has its own unique and terrifying quality. Raging water prolongs the agony: it just does not pass on by its victim after it hits them. When struck by a fierce wave one is first engulfed, then carried along with it while continuing to be battered. And, worst of all, it steals all breathable oxygen.

I was thrown upon the beach face first like a shipwrecked sailor, and while I gasped for air, the wave gently retreated back to the sea. As I choked and wiped the stinging salt from my eyes, I heard my parents comment in harmony, "We told you so."

Feeling rather intimidated and physically drained at this point, I decided to explore the shoreline. For me, combing the beach was like discovering an entirely new planet. With every breaking wave, a new creature was pushed on shore. Jellyfish, clams, fiddler crabs but the most intriguing of them all were the horseshoe crabs.

When one holds a horseshoe crab, one is holding a creature whose family tree spans over 250 million years. This living fossil gets its common name from the "U" or horseshoe shape of its shell which is called the carapace. The carapace is the color of sand or mud to help the animal blend in with its environment. Two pairs of eyes are on the rounded, front part of the carapace. These eyes are compound like those of insects. They allow the animal to see in all directions and detect movement.

A long, sharp, lance-like tail that resembles a defense weapon, sticks out from behind the horseshoe crab, but it is simply used to plow the crab through the sand, act as a rudder and right the crab when it has accidentally tipped over.

Horseshoe crabs are not crabs at all; they are related to scorpions, ticks and land spiders. Once killed to be used as fertilizer, horseshoe crabs are now under intense study within the medical profession.

In the early 1950's, scientist Frederick Bang discovered that a horseshoe crab's metallic blue-colored blood contains special cells that help kill certain kinds of bacteria. When a crab receives a wound, the cells swarm to the area to form a clot and kill the invading bacteria. Bang was able to separate the chemical in the blood cells that formed clots in the presence of bacteria.

During the summer months, horseshoe crab "Blood Drives" are conducted in the shallow waters off the Mid-Atlantic coast. After collecting blood from the crabs, they are then returned to the water. In one bay off of Cape Cod, over 80,000 crabs are bled over the course of a season. The blood is then sold for research with a price tag of up to $15,000 a quart!

Unfortunately, horseshoe crabs are being killed in record numbers for use as bait in eel and whelk fisheries off of the Atlantic coast. This has been linked to drastic declines in migratory shorebirds that feed on horseshoe crab eggs. As the crabs deposit their eggs, birds rush in and gorge themselves on this unparalleled energy source. This feast will add the fat that is critical to the birds' 6,000 mile journey from South America to their Arctic nesting grounds. In the past, the sheer enormity of the crab population ensured new generations of both birds and crabs, but this delicate balance has now been disrupted.

I picked up a frisbee-sized horseshoe crab by its dagger-like tail and placed it in my "Crayola Crayon" duffle bag. All of these new creatures fascinated me so much that I had to have them for my own.

Forewarned about jellyfish, I scooped a few of them up with my plastic sand shovel to avoid being stung, and into the bag they went. I then topped the duffle bag off with a few fiddler crabs. Knowing well that this collection would be against my parents' wishes, I concealed my treasures by laying various beach toys over them, then stuffed the bag into the spare tire compartment of our car.

As the mid-August week passed by, a "fishy" smell began to follow us everywhere. While overhearing my baffled parents guess what the odor was, I did not realize it was because of my stash.

During the five-hour drive home, the only topic of conversation was based on the awful stench. Still clueless, I simply peered out the car window and stared at the passing trees.

Several days after we had returned home, my father was about to give up his search and sell the car "**cheap, as is.**" Then I heard him yell, "RUSTY!" After hearing the tone of his voice, I paused to relish the last few seconds of not being in trouble. Then before I could respond, my father yelled from the driveway, "What in the hell is in your beach bag?"

Relieved that was all he wanted to know, I ran out to the car and said, "Oh thanks, I forgot I left them in there; I got them from the beach." As I approached, I could not understand why my father was holding my duffle bag by its drawstring with his fingertips. As he held out the "oozing" bag in front of him, he showed an awful expression on his face as if he was wishing for much longer arms. Then I realized why he was mad.

The stink was at a level above anything I have ever known. If a smell could be a form of energy, this would have been nuclear. Flies would not even approach the bag. Word has it that the flies even picketed for better working conditions. Being forced to clean out the duffle bag was enough for me to lose all interest in its contents, but I never lost my love for the ocean.

Oceans cover about 70% of the Earth's surface and contain roughly 97% of the Earth's water supply. The average ocean depth is two and a half miles with a maximum of seven miles. It was in these salty seas that life on earth first originated as a frothy foam collecting on the shores of dry land over three and a half billion years ago.

Sadly, over-exploitation of its resources has scarred our seas. Schools of fish, once assumed to be in endless abundance, are disappearing before our eyes. Every year our 1.2 million large fishing vessels return from the sea yielding smaller and smaller catches.

As marine life struggles to keep a foothold, we continue to pollute their waters. According to a report by the publishers of the *Oil Spill Intelligence Report*, approximately 32.2 million gallons of oil were spilled worldwide into the marine and inland environments during 1999 alone. The toxic chemical components of the oil can negatively affect marine life as well as physically damage their habitat.

Oceans are earth's life support system. They are at the earth's helm, controlling climate, temperature and the weather as well as producing over seventy-five percent of the planets atmospheric oxygen. They are the greatest source of clouds, yielding rain and snow that replenishes the earth's freshwater supply. Yet we have explored more of outer space than our seas.

Equally as important to the quality of our lives is the condition of all our waters. Because of their smaller size, bays, rivers, streams and lakes react much more rapidly to pollutants than an enormous ocean. Inland waters also have a higher chance of being polluted because waterfront property is considered prime real estate. And wherever we find people, we will find their garbage.

On Sept. 16, 1999, Hurricane Floyd devastated the east coast of the U.S., hitting North Carolina especially hard. Hurricane Floyd dumped 15 to 20 inches of rain and battered the North Carolina coast creating storm surges more than 10 feet high.

The majority of North Carolina's hog farms are located in the eastern third of the state in ecologically sensitive wetlands and floodplains. On these farms, millions of pounds of waste and manure are flushed out of hog barns into lagoons. Hurricane Floyd's record amounts of rainfall caused these lagoons to spill over into waterways.

Several of the environmental effects resulting from these spillovers are nitrogen and phosphorus pollution, groundwater drinking well contamination, and air pollution. Nitrogen and phosphorus pollution stimulates alga growth which robs the water of oxygen, thus killing fish and other aquatic life. The concentration of nitrates found in the local groundwater is dangerous to humans, particularly pregnant women and babies, and is associated with a number of miscarriages and "blue baby syndrome" (a disease affecting the blood's ability to absorb oxygen).

Pathogens (disease-causing organisms) such as *pfiesteria*, a toxic microorganism that kills fish and subsequently feeds off their flesh, has been associated with nitrogen and phosphorus-polluted waters. And recent studies have shown that the odor and associated air pollution from hog factories are now being linked to human health effects.

What the entire human population of most cities produce in one year, equals the amount produced by North Carolina's hogs in one day (approximately 50,000 tons of feces and urine a day). For more information on North Carolina's hog dilemma, visit www.HogWatch.org. You will also find an up-to-the-minute "Poop Counter."

With the number of chemicals in our inland waterways, communities which use them for drinking water always add chlorine to purify the water. Since, chlorine is a very active chemical, it combines with these other chemicals to form new families of chemicals, most of which are not tested for by the water facilities and are possible carcinogens.

While growing up along the Hudson River, I have sailed its waters watching many changes take place. This 315-mile long river is named after 17th century English Explorer Henry Hudson. Hudson is credited as being the first to discover the Hudson River, but many beg to differ after learning that one of Hudson's men returned from a scouting mission with an arrow through his neck.

But I suppose there were not enough arrows, because in our white man way, we moved in. Now several hundred years later we are still trying to squeeze out every tiny shred of land her banks surrender.

General Electric, the "Bring good things to life" company, dumped over two million pounds of polychlorinated biphenyl a.k.a., PCB's, into the Hudson River. The PCB's contaminated the river along with its inhabitants. PCB's are suspected to be a human carcinogen associated with liver, kidney and nervous disorders.

Fifty miles south of the GE plant, Exxon International

had been caught red-handed discharging fuel into the Hudson River. The Hudson Riverkeepers, a river watch organization, blew the whistle on this illegal activity.

750-foot Exxon oil tankers regularly departed from Aruba loaded with petroleum products such as jet fuel. After off-loading in New Jersey, the tankers would journey 90-miles up the Hudson to West Park, New York, rinse out their oil tanks, and load up on fresh water which they would use in Exxon's Aruba refinery.

In the 1970's, the General Motors plant in Tarrytown, New York, some fifty miles to the south of West Park, regularly discharged paint into the river. Fisherman setting nets near the General Motors plant could tell what color the cars were being painted that day simply by looking at the color of the water.

But to my surprise, I learned that pollution is not always an industrial crime. Many times the very people who call the river their home, are the polluters. For example, a funeral home in the city of Newburgh, New York was found discharging human blood from their "office" into the Hudson.

The thought of people desecrating the very place they live baffles me. Even dogs know enough not to soil where they sleep.

Strict regulations, ecological monitoring and, most of all, concern and action from individuals who love the river, have helped the Hudson River come a long way. Considered an open sewer in the 1960's, the Hudson now produces more fish per acre and biomass per gallon than any other major estuary in the North Atlantic. With the lower 150 miles of the Hudson as tidal estuary (a branch of the ocean), freshwater fishes such as bass, and trout, share the waters with seals, dolphin, sharks and the occasional whale. The Hudson also hosts scores of migratory species such as shad, striped bass, herring and blue-clawed crabs. Every year more and more bald eagles return to feed off the Hudson's shores. Although they were wiped out of the area from PCB's as well as other pollutants, I now have peered from my grandfather's living room window in Port Ewen, New York to see half-dozen bald eagles at once.

All inland waters are as important and sacred as the Hudson River and they all should be appreciated and protected, not only by governments, but also by the individuals living along the shores.

We humans are lucky to exist; mankind would have never graced this planet if it were not for water. No other planet in our solar system has liquid water, and what must never be forgotten is that water is the element of life. Water can exist without life, but life can not exist without water.

The Twilight of the Wild

Chapter XVII

A Thousand White Tigers in my Hand

As if sleeping, she lay peacefully on her side. Her legs were tucked in close to her body, and she still felt warm as I gently patted her on the head. Half-closed, her eyelids partially covered her ocean blue eyes and her soft creamy white fur tempted me to cuddle up next to her.

She was a 350-pound white tiger, and during the night she had peacefully died in her sleep. With approximately only 30 white tigers in the United States, an autopsy was being conducted to determine the cause of her death.

White tigers are not their own species of tiger; they are white-colored Bengal tigers. They are not albinos either;

they have a pink nose, creamy white fur with black/brown stripes, and blue eyes. White tigers only occur when two tigers mate and both carry the gene for white coloring.

I assisted the veterinarians in stretching out her nine-foot long body as the chief veterinarian made a small belly incision in order to explore her vital organs. While examining the tiger, the doctor prepared several of her vital organs for testing by sealing them in small sterilized containers. As I sat next to the tiger's head, the doctor looked up from his patient and said, "Hold this."

As if he were holding a Ming vase, the doctor carefully rested a warm fleshy sphere into my palm. "You are holding over a thousand white tigers in your hand," he said. While continuing his examination he added, "That is one of her ovaries, and it may one day save this entire species from extinction."

Mammals such as the tiger have thousands of surplus egg-cells in their ovaries, and males have millions of sperm cells in their testes. If accessed, these "gametes" as they are scientifically called, can be utilized to radically increase the breeding potential of an individual animal.

This is the future of endangered species recovery and survival. Assisted Reproduction Technology is a new conservation tool that has the potential to play a decisive role in reversing the plight of our most endangered wildlife species.

Assisted reproduction technology such as artificial insemination, embryo transfer and invitro, or test-tube fertilization represent a powerful means for the recovery, storage and use of viable gametes from both live and recently deceased animals.

Embryos produced by invitro fertilization, "test-tube tigers" for example, can be transferred to recipients of the same or closely related species, or "cryopreserved"; frozen and stored for later use. Essentially, the endangered animals are able to breed long after they die.

Organizations such as Gamete Recovery International aim to recover gametes and other biomaterials from animals which die in captivity as a conservation tool for research purposes and the maintenance of genetic diversity within threatened populations.

A network (of participating institutions such as national parks, reserves, zoos and breeding farms), has established access to the genetic material of rare and endangered species that die in their facilities.

Several South African wildlife organizations have already collected and banked biological material from cheetahs, black and white rhinos, dolphins, wild dogs and sable antelope. Through this project, viable genetic material from dead endangered wildlife is recovered and recycled back into the wild. This technology minimizes the impact that the loss of an individual member can have on the rest of its already thinning population.

Assisted reproduction technology not only has the potential of saving endangered populations, but it also preserves genetic diversity.

When an animal is rescued from extinction at the last perilous minute, only a fraction of its genetic diversity remains. Genetic diversity is what makes every individual different. Every animal that sexually reproduces contains its own personal "mix" of genes. To quote E.O. Wilson in *Biodiversity* (1988. Washington, DC: National Academy Press).

The number of genes range from about 1,000 in bacteria and 10,000 in some fungi to 700,000 or more in many flowering plants and a few animals. A typical mammal such as the house mouse has about 100,000 genes. ...If stretched out fully, the DNA would be roughly one meter long. But this molecule is invisible to the naked eye....The full information contained therein, if translated into ordinary-size letter of printed text, would just about fill all 15 editions of the Encyclopedia Britannica published since 1768.

This tremendous variation within a species allows its populations to adapt to changes in climate and local environmental conditions. In addition, genetic diversity can be critical in controlling disease.

Genetic diversity boosts American farms' total crop values by over $500 million a year. Without a constant blend of new resilient genes into our crop species, pests and diseases could quickly become rampant. Genetic diversity provides a constantly evolving defense against "invaders", more so than pesticides can provide. Over 400 species of crop pests have already developed a resistance to one or more of the pesticides used to control them.

Due to human overpopulation, many wildlife populations are becoming fragmented and spread over wide distances. Highways, fences, and buildings constructed to make our lives easier, divide animal territories.

The Florida panther, for example, is at a genetic bottleneck. Due to fragmented territory and population loss, the immigration and emigration from neighboring subspecies of mountain lions has stopped. This isolation creates little or no genetic exchange between them. Unable to refresh the gene pool, the only diversity is mutation. Mutation can be important to genetic diversity but it rarely produces positive results.

In addition to auto collisions, which account for 49% of documented Florida panther deaths, inbreeding within the species has added to the population reduction. Low semen quality, lowered fertility, and a decrease in cub survival has played a huge role in limiting the Florida panther population to only 50-60 individuals. This has also happened to the cheetah population in Africa.

The effects of Florida panther inbreeding are also clearly visible. Many panthers have kinked tails and a "cowlick", or whorl of hair in the middle of its back. These are believed to be results of recessive genes being expressed through inbreeding.

Assisted reproduction technology may be one solution to the Florida Panthers problem. Breeding the Florida panther with other cats of the species, thus freshening the gene pool, might increase their reproductive potential. This has been tested on some panthers with limited success but the potential still remains.

As for the white tiger, when the veterinarians concluded their examination they were still unable to find her cause of death. Her organs were immediately sent to a laboratory for further testing, while her ovaries were prepared for safe storage.

After my final goodbye, I gently slid my hand over the tigers soft face, forever closing her ocean blue eyes, while her countless future offspring slid into a foggy cryogenic chamber awaiting the day of their birth.

Afterward

As my life continues through the Twilight of the Wild, so will my stories. But remember, you can experience stories of your own; exploring the world is a fundamental birthright for every human, no matter how young or how old. The only essential element for any explorer is simply the passion for adventure.

Visit a zoo, a state or national park, or just sit quietly by a lake or pond and watch. The pleasure of the natural world is a combination of discovery and receptiveness. You are not likely to discover this pleasure unless you are receptive.

The right to experience the world and seek adventure within it is not limited to the privileged few holding scientific degrees and seemingly endless grants. Anyone can buy a textbook. The world is open to every individual who searches to know it. Simply walk into the woods if you search for *The Twilight of the Wild*, it will find you.

About the Author

Rusty with friends - *Zimbabwe, Africa*

Rusty Johnson has spent the last 12 years speaking to over 250 educational institutions annually, teaching and entertaining people about the wonders of the natural world. He bridges the gap between humans and the earth's wild creatures by including live animals within his programs which act as ambassadors for their wild cousins.

Rusty has pursued this approach at many diverse venues ranging from *The American Museum of Natural History, Princeton University,* and *The New York Botanical Gardens,* to *The Explorers Club, The Long Island Museum of Science,* and the *National Audubon Society.* He has assisted Jim Fowler of **Mutual of Omaha's Wild Kingdom** and his television credits include *Late Night with David Letterman*, *Live with Regis and Kathy Lee*, *The Late Show with Conan O'Brien*, and the *Today Show*.

Besides Mr. Johnson's extensive knowledge of the natural world, he has many years of first-hand expertise. He is state and federally licensed for falconry, and for the breeding and raising of protected and endangered species. He has also assisted the U.S. Fish and Wildlife service in capturing bald eagles for vital research. In 1996, at the age of 25, he was inducted into The Explorers Club.

Please feel free to contact Rusty Johnson by email at:
Rusty@Twilightofthewild.com

To order additional autographed copies of:

The Twilight of the Wild

Please send check or money order to:
Pyroclastic Publishing
P.O. Box 63
Ulster Park, New York 12487

$19.95 U.S. per copy
Sales Tax: Please add 7.75% for books shipped
to New York.

Shipping by air:
US: $4.00 for the first book and $2.00 for each
additional book.
International: $9.00 for first book and $5.00 for
each additional book.